ESSAYS
Critical and
Metacritical

Eugene Paul Nassar

RUTHERFORD ● MADISON ● TEANECK
FAIRLEIGH DICKINSON UNIVERSITY PRESS
LONDON AND TORONTO: ASSOCIATED UNIVERSITY PRESSES

Associated University Presses, Inc.
4 Cornwall Drive
East Brunswick, NJ 08816

Associated University Presses Ltd
27 Chancery Lane
London WC2A 1NF, England

Associated University Presses
2133 Royal Windsor Drive
Unit 1
Mississauga, Ontario
Canada L5J 1K5

Library of Congress Cataloging in Publication Data

Nassar, Eugene Paul.
  Essays critical and metacritical.

    Bibliography: p.
    Includes index.
    Contents: Introductory overview, on continuities—
Illusion as value, an essay on a modern poetic idea—
On the posture of exultant dualism—[etc.]
    1. Literature, Modern—History and criticism—
Addresses, essays, lectures. 2. Criticism—Addresses,
essays, lectures. I. Title.
PN710.N38 1983   809'.03   81-70955
ISBN 0-8386-3128-2

Printed in the United States of America

To Paul
who has the
"kindness in the eyes"

Contents

Preface

This book is a product of a long-standing intention and a natural outgrowth of my previous writing. That writing had been largely in the area of literary criticism. This volume comprises a series of connected essays ranging out from literary criticism into the areas of social and ethical meditation. I was aided in the preparation for these essays by a fellowship from the National Endowment for the Humanities, which enabled me to read in a less haphazard way in disciplines not my own. Not with the aim of "finding" one's metacritical context; my basic metacritical positions have been implicit in the leading ideas of my previous books. But rather to gain familiarity with language and methodology in these areas, and to assess where and to what extent one had a contribution to make.

This resultant volume may seem curious in some ways. I spent a good deal of time reading with profit Max Weber, Alfred Kroeber, and G. E. Moore, to select three obvious names, but Weber does not appear in these pages, and Kroeber and Moore appear only in footnotes. Likewise with Ernst Cassirer, Emile Durkheim, and Claude Lévi-Strauss. Yet Simone Weil and Sir Karl Popper, whom I likewise read for the first time, loom large in the book. It is so because I was looking for certain ideas, certain attitudes, critical and metacritical positions, similar to my own, and for their antagonists. And when I found them, I culled them, and quoted them here. The quotations that sprinkle the book's pages do not, however, necessarily imply a thesis too derivative or stale, as my search has been aimed at demonstrating the prevalence of somewhat neglected critical and metacritical positions in wide areas of modern thought. The essays are intended, as has been everything I have written, for the serious student of literature, but also here for the humanist—and we are all humanists—reading outside his specialty, as I am here often writing outside of mine. I make no apology for so doing. It is good to have a home, but good also to walk one's neighborhood.

It is the premise of these essays that the surest way to know the full context of a society, its motivating ideals and its continuities, is through its finest art, be it sophisticated or folk art, religious or secular. The subtlest sense of late medieval Europe is in *The Canterbury Tales* and *The Divine Comedy*, not in the medieval historical records. The having of that full context—which, it seems to me, should be the goal, not only of the literary critic, but also of the historian, the sociologist, and the philosopher—is in part in the hands of the literary critic, who must do what he can to make it available through insight and precision of statement concerning unique works of art. Much recent literary criticism is not devoted to any such goal, is not focused on the given art work, but rather tends to blur, if not obliterate, any such focus. I appeal in these essays for a return to a respect for context.

I wish to thank especially Professor Cleanth Brooks, whom I had always admired as exemplary critic but had never met. He was kind enough to read this manuscript in an earlier form, to suggest very helpful changes, and finally to recommend the manuscript for publication. Mr. Thomas Yoseloff, who accepted my first book on Wallace Stevens, came once again to my aid in helping to place this last. Portions of chapters 2, 5, and 7 have appeared in *Mosaic*, *Melus*, and the *Syracuse Scholar*, respectively, and I thank the editors of these journals for permission to reprint these pieces. I am grateful to Ms. Anne Hebenstreit and Mr. Donald Yelton for their careful editing of the typescript and to Mrs. Magdalene Seiselmyer for her cheerful retyping of the various drafts.

Utica College of Syracuse University
Utica, New York

ESSAYS
Critical and Metacritical

1
Introductory Overview: On Continuities

These essays are intended primarily as a further exploration of ideas concerning criticism and metacriticism put forward in my *The Rape of Cinderella: Essays in Literary Continuity*. The argument there is that "criticism" ought to be defined as the accurate response to the unique "tone" (or, body of attitudes) of a work and the continuity of that tone. The emphasis in that volume and in all of my previous writing has been on close analysis of contextual continuities, which are created and communicated by unique detail.

I hinted, however, in the *Cinderella* volume, especially in the chapter entitled "Metacriticism," that so long as the critic is clear when he is performing the critical act and when not, he need not repress the, in any case almost irresistible, impulse to speculate on the possible relations of his ideas, aesthetic or other, to the vast world of speculation on life-in-general. I hinted too then the direction my own speculations would naturally take: to argue that continuity in life may be a fundamental desire of the human spirit, that "continuity" may be considered a first principle of value in experience as well as a first principle of evaluation in criticism.

We may hunger more, that is, for order than truth . . . for illusion rather than contrariety, more for the unique imaginative world of an individual spirit than for existential poise in the face of an irresolvable dualism. And then too there is always the religious

13

question as to whether "illusion" might not in fact, be "vision."
(P. 139)

These essays will attempt to elaborate upon these assertions, to argue for the ultimate "necessity" to hold to some
context of values and beliefs, to assumptions that will give
meaning and continuity to one's life. These contexts, these
assumptions, cannot be supplied by science, and are no less
necessary for not being subject to scientific proof or disproof.
Such contexts I would further argue must be seen as irreducible with respect to their details, for the detail *is* the context.

I would argue these positions now, in part because the aesthetic ideas of continuity and contextualism aid, I feel, in the
study of social, ethical, and religious contexts, but also, and
reflexively, because, if persuasive in these broader areas of
thought, these ideas reinvigorate our sense of why supreme art
is of great importance to modern man. These ideas would
stress that the continuity of a "poem" partially satisfies the
hunger for social continuity, which partially satisfies the hunger for personal continuity, that is, for an immortality which
includes the unique detail of our personal contexts. It is supreme art which dramatizes these loved, unique contexts, and
it is close critical analysis, precision in the handling of unique
detail, which aids in making clear the given cherished context.

I want in the early essays of this book to do both some
critical probing into, and some metacritical musing about, the
works of various writers. The later essays in the areas of social
and ethical questions, aside from whatever contributions they
may or may not make, will exhibit their origins in the critical
and metacritical positions of the previous book and the antece-
dent chapters.

The first two essays attempt a synopsis of two philosophic
positions current in the cultural air since the Romantic movement, especially in the twentieth century, but only dimly
articulated in the literature on "intellectual currents." The
positions are embraced by the catch-phrases "illusion as value"
and "exultant dualism." With the first I have a good deal of

sympathy, with the second not much, for reasons critical and intrinsic as well as metacritical and extrinsic.

The first position constitutes the explicit and implicit poetics of Wallace Stevens, but also, as I shall try to show in chapter 2, is the implicit and often explicit poetics of other major twentieth-century poets such as Robert Frost, William Butler Yeats, William Carlos Williams, Hart Crane, and Ezra Pound. It is in fact a major position, philosophic and aesthetic, in the modern culture of the West. Yet it has not been accorded by cultural historians the major status its prevalence warrants. The cultural situation metaphysically of the twentieth-century West is still formulated in the nineteenth-century categories of faith vs. unbelief, true enough as ultimate categories, but imprecise in their blurring the fact of the "coming of age" of the position traced in chapter 2, a position not acceptable as a major hypothesis before the Romantic movement.

The most explicit exposition of the root ideas of illusion as value is in Hans Vaihinger's *The Philosophy of "As If"*:

> The imaginary (the absolute, ideal) is therefore justifiable in spite of its unreality. Without the imaginary factor neither science nor life in their highest form are possible. The real tragedy of life is that the most valuable ideas are, from the point of view of reality, worthless. The value of reality is thus reversed. F. A. Lange has also pointed out that the ideal and the real interchange their roles; that the ideal, the unreal, is the most valuable: that men must "demand the impossible," even if it leads to contradictions.
>
> . . . Thus, according to Kant, man is not merely to be judged in his conduct *as if* he were a free agent, but should conduct himself *as if*, at some time or other, he were to be held accountable for his acts. . . .
>
> All the nobler aspects of our life are based upon fictions. We have already contended that a *pure ethic* can only be established by the recognition of its fictional basis. How closely truth and illusion thus approach one another is apparent. We shall have occasion in the sequel to point out how "truth" is really merely the most expedient type of error. It is an error to suppose that an absolute truth, an absolute criterion of knowledge and behaviour,

can be discovered. The higher aspects of life are based upon noble delusions. (Pp. 44, 47, 84)

Depressing, though not as depressing as despair or nihilism, and a basis, such as it is, for idealisms, without which, Vaihinger says, man cannot live. The American reader will sense in the remarks of Vaihinger a good deal of Santayana:

> This higher plane is the sphere of significant imagination, of relevant fiction. . . . Poetry raised to its highest power is then identical with religion grasped in its inmost truth; at their point of union both reach their utmost purity and beneficence, for then poetry loses its frivolity and ceases to demoralize, while religion surrenders its illusions and ceases to deceive. (*Interpretations of Poetry and Religion*, [1900] p. 290)

The Spanish reader, a good deal of Unamuno:

> Nevertheless, yes, we must needs long for it [personal immortality], however absurd it may appear to us; nay, more, we must needs believe in it, in some way or another, in order that we may live. (*The Tragic Sense of Life*, [1921] p. 257)

Vaihinger traces the idea of "necessary" or "useful" "fictions" from Kant, especially, to F. A. Lange, and finally to Nietzsche's sense of man's tragic dilemma:

> The erroneousness of a concept does not for me constitute an objection to it; the question is—to what extent is it advantageous to life. . . . Indeed I am convinced that *the most erroneous assumptions are precisely the most indispensable for us*, that without granting the validity of the logical *fiction*, without measuring reality by the invented world . . . man could not live; and that a negation of this fiction . . . is equivalent to a negation of life itself. To admit untruth as a condition of life—this does indeed imply a terrible negation of the customary valuations. (*The Philosophy of "As If,"* pp. 354–55; quoted from Nietzsche's *Werke*, vol. 14, p. 16; italics are Vaihinger's)

One can recognize the same tortured idea in Ivan Karamazov's extension of himself in the Grand Inquisitor:

. . . but isn't that suffering, at least for a man like that, who has wasted his whole life in the desert and yet could not shake off his incurable love of humanity? In his old age he reached the clear conviction that nothing but the advice of the great dread spirit could build up any tolerable sort of life for the feeble, unruly, "incomplete, empirical creatures created in jest." And so, convinced of this, he sees that he must follow the counsel of the wise spirit, the dread spirit of death and destruction, and therefore accept lying and deception, and lead men consciously to death and destruction, and yet deceive them all the way so that they may not notice where they are being led, that the poor blind creatures may at least on the way think themselves happy. And note, the deception is in the name of Him in Whose ideal the old man had so fervently believed all his life long. Is not that tragic?[1] (*The Brothers Karamazov*, p. 321)

And later in Conrad's *Heart of Darkness:*

"'Yes, I know,' I said with something like despair in my heart, but bowing my head before the faith that was in her, before that great and saving illusion that shone with an unearthly glow in the darkness, in the triumphant darkness from which I could not have defended her—from which I could not even defend myself. (p. 601)

The idea of the necessity of cultivating the heart's needs rather than "Truth" is not so tragic to Conrad or to William James as it was for Nietzsche or Dostoevski. James uses the argument of Pascal's wager to combat the skepticism of "Science," in his famous essay "The Will to Believe" (1896):

The talk of believing by our volition seems, then, from one point of view, simply silly. From another point of view it is worse than silly, it is vile. . . . It is only natural that those who have caught the scientific fever should pass over to the opposite extreme, and write sometimes as if the incorruptibly truthful intellect ought positively to prefer bitterness and unacceptableness to the heart in its cup. . . . Science can tell us what exists; but to compare the *worths*, both of what exists and of what does not exist, we must consult not science, but what Pascal calls our heart. Science herself consults her heart when she lays it down that the infinite ascertainment of fact and correction of false belief are the supreme goods for man. . . . Our belief in truth itself, for instance, that there is a truth, and that our minds and it are made for each other,—what is it but a passionate affirmation of desire. . . . Dupery for dupery, what proof is there that dupery through hope is so much worse than dupery through fear? I, for one, can see no proof; and I simply refuse obedience to the scientist's command to imitate his kind of option, in a case where my own stake is important enough to give me the right to choose my own form of risk . . . my willingness to run the risk of acting as if my passional need of taking the world religiously might be prophetic and right. (*Essays on Faith and Morals*, pp. 38, 40, 53, 58)

James's position however is not quite that of illusion as value, but, rather, culminates in a theism:

I myself believe, of course, that the religious hypothesis gives to the world an expression which specifically determines our reactions, and makes them in a large part unlike what they might be on a purely naturalistic scheme of belief. (p. 61)

I suppose that my belief that in communion with the Ideal new force comes into the world, and new departures are made here below, subjects me to being classed among the supernaturalists of the . . . crasser type. . . .

The further limits of our being plunge, it seems to me, into an altogether other dimension of existence from the sensible and merely 'understandable' world. Name it the mystical region, or the supernatural region, whichever you choose. (*The Varieties of Religious Experience*, "Conclusions" and "Postscript," pp. 515, 521)

I find such a will to believe and such a theism resonant in my own spirit, and a good deal of my own metacritical thought has been influenced, I am sure, by James. Also by Dostoevski, by Unamuno, by T. S. Eliot, and, to be sure, by a number of others. I was pleased to find resonant theist positions in, though I found them too late to be much influenced by, Simone Weil and Teilhard de Chardin, both of whom adopt at crucial points in their thinking the "either-or" posture of Pascal, James, Dostoevski, Unamuno, Eliot, and of much other modern theistic thought:

For the last two or three centuries, people have believed that force rules supreme over all natural phenomena, and at the same time that men can and should base their mutual relations upon justice, recognized as such through the application of reason. This is a flagrant absurdity. . . .

There is only one possible choice to be made. Either we must perceive at work in the universe, alongside force, a principle of a different kind, or else we must recognize force as being the unique and sovereign ruler over human relations also. (Simone Weil, *The Need for Roots*, p. 241)

Between these two alternatives of absolute optimism or absolute pessimism, there is no middle way. . . .

We are confronted accordingly with two directions and only two: one upwards and the other downwards, and there is no possibility of finding a halfway house. (Teilhard de Chardin, *The Phenomenon of Man*, p. 232)

I quote from these examples at hand to delineate clearly and early positions which underlie my own metacritical speculations in these essays. Other and perhaps more real influences might have been summoned up from one's past, but I think to no special purpose.

The "or" option of the atheist, the existential world-without-God, comprises, of course, a position of enormous force in the modern world. Aesthetically, the theist or atheist positions have no more or less legitimacy than their tonal continuity gives them in a given unique context. One looks at the phenomenological real, full of apparent dualisms and antinomies, and then, in his art or thought, one makes clear whether he intends to dramatize the dualisms, the antinomies, or to dramatize instead his beliefs, hopes, dreams of a unity beyond the dualisms. The critic assesses the given work as drama, by its continuity, its inner richness of tone.[2]

The position which I call "exultant dualism" in chapter 3 and which I find discontinuous, aesthetically, psychologically, tonally, is one easy to slip into, and one into which most thinkers, the better and the worse, seem sometimes to slip. It is the blurring, the dissolving of the problem by denying its existence or pretending it is no problem. When all seems unity to the psychology, it is tempting to deny the dualisms, or, worse, to call evil somehow good. Theists and atheists do this all the time, attempting to pass their moments of psychic uplift as full satisfaction for the human hunger for a continuum of such moments, for permanence and immortality. It is a matter of tact and precision. Eliot's belief never loses the tact and the tonal continuity of presenting his religious moments as but fitful illuminations in darkness:

> There is no end of it, the voiceless wailing,
> No end to the withering of withered flowers,
> To the movement of pain that is painless and motionless,
> To the drift of the sea and the drifting wreckage,
> The bone's prayer to Death its God. Only the hardly, barely prayable
> Prayer of the one Annunciation.
>
> (*Four Quartets*, "The Dry Salvages" 2:79–84)

Nor does Santayana's unbelief ever lose the tact of recognition that reason cannot satisfy man's passional needs:

> Each must sometimes fall back upon the soul; . . . he must ask himself for the mainspring and value of his life. He will then remember his stifled loves; he will feel that only his illusions have ever given him a sense of reality, only his passions the hope and the vision of peace. (*Interpretations of Poetry and Religion*, p. 268)

The aesthetic argument with the posture of exultant dualism is not of course with the transcendental experience, the euphoric moment, but with the tone of arrogance (no different from the tone of arrogance so often in belief or unbelief), the pretense, the inadequacy in dramatic presentation, and the cloaking of small victories in the trappings of empire. Chapter 3 attempts to show how the slipping into the posture hurts the continuity of the work of some major artists since the Romantic movement. Chapter 8 later attempts to broaden the scope of the analysis to show how the tendency of mind to dissolve hard realities exhibits itself in various areas of modern life, manifesting the same arrogance, imprecision of analysis, and avoidance of unique context and tone in favor either of the proliferation of categories or archetypes or of a single, monist category of categories—twists at opposite ends of the same rope.

Chapter 7 attempts to outline a philosophy of contextual continuity, to probe, as I have said, the applicability of ideas of tone and continuity in unique aesthetic contexts to social contexts, of what I consider the principles of criticism of aesthetic orders to unique social orders. Chapters 4, 5, and 6 constitute essays mainly "critical"; each chapter however contains some metacritical ruminations arising out of the analysis which relate to the leading metacritical ideas of this book.

These ideas flow, I feel, naturally from the aesthetic ideas of tone and continuity. These ideas—mere operations of the rational life—do not attempt to resolve antinomies; only faith can do that. But (to use a metaphor from Pound's *Cantos*), as the crystal gem with its internal clarity can serve as the impossible ideal of the continuous art work, so can it serve as the ideal (though never the reality) of the continuous society. Clarity and continuity within a society need imply no metaphysical continuity without; thus the leading idea of this book is pluralistic. And any rock can of course be cohesive without giving light; thus the leading idea of this book, the aesthetic and ethical principle of continuity, is to be seen as but a necessary, though not sufficient, principle of the good work or the good life.

The human need for stability and order *can*, to be sure, petrify into a stagnant, intolerant tyranny. The evaluation of the quality of an art work or a social context depends first on the critical act, on the accurate grasp of the central attitudes (the "tone") of the given context and the continuity of these. But the final judgement of the work or the society's value to the observer will depend on a metacritical assessment, on the observer's personal values.

The need for continuity in art and in life may provide a basis for comparisons between metacritical positions. Implicit throughout this book is the suggestion that the hunger for continuity may be a bedrock principle of the mind, and so serve as the linking idea between the areas of criticism and metacriticism. But then again it may not.

Chapter 9 therefore attempts but a summary statement of what is stressed in each chapter: that only by the cultivation of the attributes of tolerance, humility, and sympathy, the detailed and precise understanding of others, the close analysis of the springs of other continuities and contexts, and by the harnessing of the opposite tendencies, arrogant monomania, hatred, intolerance, imprecise knowledge and broad-brush categorizations of others, can human beings and human societies allow for the myriad loves that may be illusions, the myriad beauties that may not be true. One needs to so allow, since one's own beauty, one's own love, may be but one of the many.

Notes

1. Plato's "noble lie" in *The Republic*, bk. 3, is a similar conception in a nontragic context.

2. See my *The Rape of Cinderella*, chap. 10, "The Critical Act," pp. 127–29, on this approach.

2
Illusion as Value: An Essay on a Modern Poetic Idea

> To speak of the whole world as metaphor
> Is still to stick to the contents of the mind
>
> And the desire to believe in a metaphor.
> It is to stick to the nicer knowledge of
> Belief, that what it believes in is not true.
>> Wallace Stevens, "The Pure Good of Theory"

Criticism ought to be the art or act of responding with precision to the subtlest tonalities of a unique work of art. Most of what is in fact called criticism in our time (as in all times) is "metacriticism," the comparing of the "critic's" sense of value with the author's, or, worse, the hunting for the critic's outside interests in the poet's texts. It is evident that a metacritical posture in a reader or body of readers can blur the critical response and the attempt at precision. It has been my experience in reading and writing about modern poetry that all sorts of metacritical postures have intruded into the precise examination of the actual attitudes of various poets in various poems. At the same time, the ever-present tendency to categorize and pigeonhole in "criticism" has caused all sorts of superficial distinctions to be made between certain poets who in fact share a sense of the world and the human condition and its solaces far more significant than the distinctions.

And if it continues to be true, as it has always been true in the past, that the major poets of a period take on more and more importance as cultural representatives of a period as decades and centuries pass, it is then no mere academic exercise to struggle for as much objective precision in the articulation of the attitudes of major modern poets as criticism can manage. The idea expressed in its baldest form in the Stevens passage above—the idea of illusion as value—*is* a central attitude in much of modern poetry. It is so because it is a natural response of an artistic temperament to the modern world—a response not necessarily natural to temperaments philosophically, historically, sociologically, or even critically, oriented. It is a metacriticism of life held by poets who do not share the metacritical postures of many critics of their art. I hope in this essay to be critically just to the poets whose unique texts and contexts I examine, while at the same time presenting the important though critically neglected attitude toward reality and art shared by these modern poets.

To believe in poetry, in art, in objects of beauty, in products of an ordering imagination, while at the same time realizing that it is only a "pretend" belief summoned up by the desire, the vast human hunger for belief, and to feel that perceived reality fosters no such belief—such are the basic attitudes of Wallace Stevens and of the stream of thought in modern poetry which I wish to trace:

> These leaves are the poem, the icon and the man.
> These are a cure of the ground and of ourselves,
>
> In the predicate that there is nothing else.
> ("The Rock," Sec. 2)

The leaves figure both the leaves of spring which cover the barren rock of reality and the leaves of works of poetry which invest our lives with value "in the predicate that there is nothing else." Leaves do not really grow on rock however, and the imagination's created world is figured as a child's dreaming:

> It is a child that sings itself to sleep,
> The mind, among the creatures that it makes,
> The people, those by which it lives and dies.
> ("The Owl in the Sarcophagus")

It is thus that the life of the mind is an "inescapable romance, inescapable choice/Of dreams, disillusion as the last illusion."[1] "Inescapable" because necessary as a self-defense against meaninglessness: "disillusion" therefore as but a stage in one's course toward a new illusion. And thus it is that Stevens constructs what he can of blessedness out of the "pleasures of merely circulating" from fiction to fiction. For the modern "natives of poverty" Stevens has only the "gaiety of language" as substitute for the "seigneur,"[2] the transcendental absolute God that gave value to an earlier world.

> Place-bound and time-bound in evening rain
> And bound by a sound which does not change,
>
> Except that it begins and ends,
> Begins again and ends again—
>
> Rain without change within or from
> Without. In this place and in this time
>
> And in this sound, which do not change,
> In which the rain is all one thing,
>
> In the sky, an imagined, wooden chair
> Is the clear-point of an edifice,
>
> Forced up from nothing, evening's chair,
> Blue-strutted curule, true—unreal,
>
> The centre of transformations that
> Transform for transformation's self,
>
> In a glitter that is a life, a gold
> That is a being, a will, a fate.
>
> ("Human Arrangement")

The chair (an imperial chair, the poet's chair of meditation) is forced up into the sky by the poet's will to escape the meaningless rain. It is the sad thrust of what Stevens calls the "rage for order" in the poem "The Idea of Order at Key

West," the same desire ("true—unreal") which in the Key West poem manages the unmanageable ocean through song.

These basic attitudes toward reality and art are perhaps dismal enough, but they are the root attitudes for Stevens's transformations, and are beneath the gaiety and bravura of surface in much of his early poetry. The first generation of Stevens criticism tended to attack him for frivolity, the later generation to put him into a quasi-transcendental, untragic context. The precise tonality of Stevens's poetry is neither frivolous nor romantic-transcendental, but is centered on the idea of illusion as value.[3] Much of the poetry which I examine below, while similarly centered, has, for various reasons, been similarly misrepresented.

Too many people knew and were fascinated by the life of Hart Crane, and the wildly disparate criticism of his great poem, *The Bridge*, has flowed mainly from extrinsic facts and considerations rather than from precise examination of its intrinsic effects of language. That language, often attacked as confused or intoxicated, is in fact a subtle and precise dramatization of complex attitudes that revolve around the idea of illusion as value. The three sections of *The Bridge* most often labeled as incoherent by hostile criticism are those entitled "Atlantis," "Cape Hatteras," and "The Dance"; I want to examine a passage from each.

The spiritual "traveler" in *The Bridge*, the man, like Crane sensitive to the past and baffled by the present (one "Jason" in the long line), is he who

> Searches the timeless laugh of mythic spears.
>
> Like hails, farewells—up planet-sequined heights
> Some trillion whispering hammers glimmer Tyre:
> Serenely, sharply up the long anvil cry
> Of inchling aeons silence rivets Troy.
> And you, aloft there—Jason! hesting Shout!
> Still wrapping harness to the swarming air!
> Silvery the rushing wake, surpassing call,
> Beams yellow AEolus! splintered in the straights!
>
>   ("Atlantis")

The "timeless laugh of mythic spears" refers to the necessary sufficiency of myth, like the *Iliad* of Greek myth, to delight the spirit of man which eternally hungers for myth. Myth-making is like sequining planets—part lie and absurd, but it is too like the instinct of self-preservation in us all: "trillion whispering hammers glimmer Tyre." We hail the myth of Tyre we thus fashion (rivet) as we bid others, like that of Troy, farewell. Cyclically ("cycloramically" is Crane's apt word) mankind (Jason the traveler) "harnesses the air," forges something of nothing (AEolus from silver beams of light on water), eventually to be "splintered in the straights." The language in which these attitudes are expressed, it should be seen, is not gratuitously odd but carefully poised (words, phrases, and ideas of affirmation balanced against those of pain and tragedy) to wrench full poignancy (anvil cry) out of the tragic situation, to express the total implications of man's dependence on mythologies that do not survive. These attitudes are not an answer to anything; they are a dramatization of a felt dualism that is made bearable by the inventions (shared or personal) of the imagination:

> The nasal whine of power whips a new universe . . .
> Towards what?—
> Stars scribble on our eyes the frosty sagas,
> The gleaming cantos of unvanquished space . . .
> What ciphers risen from prophetic script,
> What marathons new-set between the stars! . . .
> New latitudes, unknotting, soon give place
> To what fierce schedules, rife of doom apace!
>
> ("Cape Hatteras")

The essential vision of these lines and the ground vision of the poem is that history is directionless, a cyclic unknotting of new doomed mythic universes. Mankind weaves warm myths, sagas, cantos of cold ever-unvanquished space, sets new marathons up in the old stars, there where man has placed many other such in human history.

So then when the reader is presented with a symbolic rendering of a modern condition by a poet of this sophistication using motifs from American Indian myth, he should not, as so many critics have, postulate a Crane of confused, rather pitiful mystic gesturings:

> Sprout, horn!
> Spark, tooth! Medicine-man, relent, restore—
> Lie to us,—dance us back the tribal morn!
>
> ("The Dance")

The poetic consciousness that asks the "medicine man"— primitive poet—to "lie to us" is decidedly unprimitive. The request is sad and represents the tragically mixed blessing of illusion and myth in a sophisticated consciousness. The dance is representative of the mind's (man's) circular motions, getting nowhere but where one needs emotionally to be. *The Bridge* keeps running variations on this idea of a never-ending cyclic movement from reality to myth, from tragedy to illusion and back again. This movement is the poem's form and theme and key to its linguistic effects.[4]

W. H. Auden articulates often a kindred sense of life:

> Not to be born is the best for man;
> The second-best is a formal order,
> The dance's pattern: Dance while you can.
>
> ("O Who Can Ever Gaze His Fill")

Such is Death's reply in a debate with fishermen, travelers, lovers, and dreamers. The implication is of course that all formal orders may be but sanctuaries of illusion from a despair in a disordered reality.

> Asleep in our huts, how we dream of a part
> In the glorious balls of the future; each intricate maze
> Has a plan, and the disciplined movements of the heart
> Can follow for ever and ever its harmless ways.
>
> ("In Time of War")

The irony of the "glorious balls" image is no less clear than the pathos of our hunger for an aristocratic sense of ourselves. The same irony, the same pathos, obtains in the attitude of the lover in the exquisite "Lay Your Sleeping Head, My Love," who believes in nothing ("Beauty, midnight, vision dies") and wants to believe in everything, for, as he says in "September 1, 1939," "We must love one another or die." Similarly in the attitude of the narrator of "In Praise of Limestone," who mocks the limited, ordered society of any group of common humanity (figured in the malleable, variegated, limestone landscape) while confessing in the closing lines that he can see nothing lovely that is not compounded of common humanity. It is man's constructs that make him human; his dreams are the basis of his blessed ability to love, and so too the basis for his tragedy and anxiety.

This is all close to the sense of life in Stevens and Crane, save that Auden never stayed fixed in the area of meditation on art and myth, but ranged into the areas of politics, social action, and finally, religion. It has been fashionable to find Auden a bit glib and unsteady, but there is in Auden that central continuity of attitude that belies such criticism: the attitude that we *must* find bases for love, illusory or no. Of course there are other answers: Auden's own later religious commitment, Eliot's also, and every sort of transcendental belief to humanistic unbelief. But these latter have always been with us; the newer phenomenon is the acceptability of the idea that what we most love may be illusions purely self-generated and yet none the less valuable or necessary.

It is that idea which is implied in Yeats's famous phrase "the ceremony of innocence":

> How but in custom and in ceremony
> Are innocence and beauty born?
> ("A Prayer for My Daughter")

"Custom" and "ceremony" refer to tradition, rituals, patterns, orders, beliefs, beauty of the past. "Innocence" is used in three different senses in this poem, all relevant to the thrust of this essay. There is first the innocence of the poet's child sleeping in the cradle. There is then the "murderous innocence" of the howling sea—the blank neutrality of nature.

Finally there is the "radical innocence" which the adult suffering soul recovers when it recognizes in a harsh modern reality
that it is "self-delighting/Self-appeasing, self-affrighting."
This is not the innocence of the peasant who believes in his
ceremonies and rituals with a simple, childlike faith, but a
soul's commitment to order and beauty despite the following
tragic realization:

> We were the last romantics—chose for theme
> Traditional sanctity and loveliness;
> Whatever's written in what poets name
> The book of the people; whatever most can bless
> The mind of man or elevate a rhyme;
> But all is changed, that high horse riderless,
> Though mounted in that saddle Homer rode
> Where the swan drifts upon a darkening flood.
>
> ("Coole and Ballylee")

What is gone for the poet and the people is the loveliness of
living and working within a tradition one can believe in and
which can lend value to our lives. The poet is left in our
century with the realization that "Whatever flames upon the
night/Man's own resinous heart has fed," so that man's ideals
become "self-born mockers of man's enterprise."[5]
   Yet the modern poet endures this tragic vision, as the illusions of art create a haven from the fury of the ocean of reality:

> Marbles of the dancing floor
> Break bitter furies of complexity,
> Those images that yet
> Fresh images beget,
> That dolphin-torn, that gong-tormented sea.
>
> ("Byzantium")

Byzantium represents the temporary solaces of the realm of
art (the ever-vital image, the dance, the golden bird, the flame
of the creative imagination) within chaotic reality (furies of
complexity, mire and blood, death and time as fire and ocean).
To sail to Byzantium is nothing like escaping for long the

irreducible tragedy of human life, as the poet's poignant cry demonstrates:

> Consume my heart away; sick with desire
> And fastened to a dying animal
> It knows not what it is; and gather me
> Into the artifice of eternity.
>
> ("Sailing to Byzantium")

That is, the desire for permanence of life or life after death never wanes; the artificial eternities of the products of the creative imagination are all the poet asks for. That the poet wants so very much more, that the illusions of art are the values he must *settle* for, these attitudes have always been clear to me in the lines. But I find much of the criticism on Yeats taking literally figurations that Yeats the poet meant only symbolically: Yeats appreciated Blake and Shelley and therefore he is to be explained by a Blakean or Shelleyan neo-Platonism, or whatever; Yeats the man dabbles with Blavatskian spiritualism or with Rosicrucianism, or whatever; therefore cabalistic iconography is the last word on Yeats. Whatever the man's casting about, Yeats the poet always and obsessively, it seems to me, wrote from the posture of the modern man who, tragically, could have no literal belief in ideals, values, rituals he passionately loved:

> Civilisation is hooped together, brought
> Under a rule, under the semblance of peace
> By manifold illusion
>
> ("Meru")

The poems early and late center around the temporary solaces of beauty in the tragic landscape. Witness the Chinamen who climb the mountain in the late poem "Lapis Lazuli":

> There, on the mountain and the sky,
> On all the tragic scene they stare.
> One asks for mournful melodies;
> Accomplished fingers begin to play.

> Their eyes mid many wrinkles, their eyes,
> Their ancient, glittering eyes, are gay.

It is a "gaiety" in this poem like the "innocence" of the poem to his daughter—a gaiety within tragedy which has wrought its "uttermost," within the vision of reality as endless dualism and disorder.[6] It is the irreducible power of art, of illusion. So strong is the desire for value, meaning, things to love and believe in, that in the absence of any evidence, man will create his own dark mysteries in gazing at a statue of "empty eye-balls" and mathematically (unmysteriously) calculated proportions:

> We Irish, born into that ancient sect
> But thrown upon this filthy modern tide
> And by its formless spawnings fury wrecked,
> Climb to our proper dark, that we may trace
> The lineaments of a plummet-measured face.
>
> ("The Statues")

That "ancient sect" are those with a hunger to believe, who down through human history have climbed into the dark out of the light of reality, to the place where they need to be. Poignant? Yes. Absurd? No.

Imprecision in the critical handling of Robert Frost's poetry was the subject of a brilliant ground-clearing essay by Randall Jarrell in his *Poetry and the Age* (1953). Jarrell's "other Frost," the Frost of the dark vision of man's existential condition, is the true Frost at the tonal center of his work, not the Frost of the journalists of a popular culture. But that revision, that making more accurate the old inaccurate view of Frost, is fairly established now. What is yet to be firmly established is Frost's sense of value within that darker vision. And it is with Frost, as with the other poets of this essay, that the idea of illusion as value is central:

> The people along the sand
> All turn and look one way.
> They turn their back on the land.
> They look at the sea all day.

> As long as it takes to pass
> A ship keeps raising its hull;
> The wetter ground like glass
> Reflects a standing gull.
>
> The land may vary more;
> But wherever the truth may be—
> The water comes ashore,
> And the people look at the sea.
>
> They cannot look out far.
> They cannot look in deep.
> But when was that ever a bar
> To any watch they keep?
> ("Neither Out Far Nor in Deep")

One couldn't be more wrong than to feel that Frost is not with these people, that the poet would have the people turn their backs to the sea and start exploring the land behind them. This little poem is symbolic of the irrepressible metaphysical longing, the hunger for knowledge of origins and destinies and for values based on that knowledge. The knowledge of the land is of no such things. Most of Frost's poetry is of knowledge of the land, but this very knowledge is what turns man to the sea, or, inland, to the sea's tributaries:

> And if you're lost enough to find yourself
> By now, pull in your ladder road behind you
> And put a sign up CLOSED to all but me.
> Then make yourself at home. The only field
> Now left's no bigger than a harness gall.
> First there's the children's house of make believe,
> Some shattered dishes underneath a pine,
> The playthings in the playhouse of the children.
> Weep for what little things could make them glad.
> Then for the house that is no more a house. . . .
> Your destination and your destiny's
> A brook that was the water of the house . . .
> I have kept hidden in the instep arch
> Of an old cedar at the waterside
> A broken drinking goblet like the Grail

> Under a spell so the wrong ones can't find it,
> So can't get saved, as Saint Mark says they mustn't.
> (I stole the goblet from the children's playhouse.)
> Here are your waters and your watering place.
> Drink and be whole again beyond confusion.
>
> ("Directive")

The waters of salvation are in the origins of the child's world of make believe, i.e., the imagination. All reality fades, all that is left is the individual's memory and the individual desire to recapture the feelings of wholeness and order and purpose. The poet in this poem leads us back to humble, pathetic and yet all-important origins and ends: the imagination and its dreams. For it is the imagination's meditations on origins ("backward motion"), which fight against reality (the ongoing stream), that makes human life valuable:

> It is this backward motion toward the source,
> Against the stream, that most we see ourselves in,
> The tribute of the current to the source.
> It is from this in nature we are from.
> It is most us.
>
> ("West-running Brook")

The brook runs "westward" (life to death), though it is the eddy against the brook's direction that we revere:

> The universal cataract of death
> That spends to nothingness—and unresisted,
> Save by some strange resistance in itself,
> Not just a swerving, but a throwing back,
> As if regret were in it and were sacred.

It seems to the romantic lady in the dialogue that the white eddy is waving to the couple, but the lady's lover protests realistically that it was always thus: "It wasn't waved to us." The lady answers:

> It wasn't, yet it was. If not to you
> It was to me—in an annunciation.

The religious evocation, here as in the Grail and St. Mark passage above, is apt in that the "will to believe," the "strange resistance," the "throwing back," is sacred in its lending love and light and value to human life. The "annunciation" may or may not be more than illusion (the phrase is, "as if"), but, no matter, it is "most us."

No reader has been able to miss, as they have often missed in Frost, the stark and dark reality in the poetry of William Carlos Williams, but what has not been emphasized nearly enough is his immense sympathy for what he plainly considers the human illusions ("lullaby") necessary to endure that reality.

> Go to sleep—though of course you will not—
> to tideless waves thundering slantwise against
> strong embankments, rattle and swish of spray
> dashed thirty feet high, . . .
>
> Gentlefooted crowds are treading out your lullaby,
> Their arms nudge, they brush shoulders,
> hitch this way, then that, mass and surge at the crossings—
> lullaby, lullaby! The wild-fowl police whistles,
> the enraged roar of the traffic, machine shrieks:
> it is all to put you to sleep.
>
> It is the sting of snow, the burning liquor of
> the moonlight, the rush of rain in the gutters packed
> with dead leaves: go to sleep, go to sleep.
> And the night passes—and never passes—
>
> ("A Goodnight")

The "night" of the spirit, here described, is the awake nightmare, the despair, the coldness, emptiness within reality, the "mine" of loneliness.

> In this mine they come to dig—all.
> Is this the counterfoil to sweetest
>
> music? The source of poetry that
> seeing the clock stopped, says,
> The clock has stopped

that ticked yesterday so well?
and hears the sound of lakewater
splashing—that is now stone.

                                                                    ("These")

The "source of poetry" is the struggle of the will first to iden-
tify and then to fight in self-defense against modern paralysis,
modern despair. It is the mind's hearing of lakewater splash
where there is only stone in reality; it is to "sleep and dream,"
to think of flowers and rivers as one looks at pain and suffering:

IT IS MYSELF,
          not the poor beast lying there
                    yelping with pain
     that brings me to myself with a start—
               as at the explosion
                    of a bomb, a bomb that has laid
     all the world waste.
               I can do nothing
                    but sing about it
     and so I am assuaged
               from my pain.
A DROWSY NUMBNESS drowns my sense
               as if of hemlock
                    I had drunk, I think
     of the poetry
               of René Char
                    and all he must have seen
     and suffered
               that has brought him
                    to speak only of
     sedgy rivers,
               of daffodils and tulips
                    whose roots they water,
     even to the freeflowing river
               that laves the rootlets
                    of those sweet scented flowers
     that people the
               milky
                    way.
                         ("To a Dog Injured in the Street")

The mind of René Char created its own ordered universe (flowers in the milky way) that is clearly not inclusive of modern objective reality (world-wasting bomb). So that when Williams ends his poem with

> René Char,
>   you are a poet who believes
>   in the power of beauty
>   to right all wrongs.
>   I believe it also.
> With invention and courage
>   we shall surpass
>   the pitiful dumb beasts,
>   let all men believe it,
>   as you have taught me also
>   to believe it.

—it is clear how very sad and minimal (no less necessary) this apparently rousingly romantic statement really is in context. It is in the mind only that wrongs are righted by beauty.

That is late Williams, and this is even later:

>   It is the mind
>   the mind
>   that must be cured
>   short of death's
>   intervention,
>   and the will becomes again
>   a garden. The poem
> is complex and the place made
>   in our lives
>   for the poem.
> Silence can be complex too,
>   but you do not get far
>   with silence.
> Begin again.
>   It is like Homer's
>   catalogue of ships:
> it fills up the time. . . .
>   Love
>   to which you too shall bow

```
          along with me—
               a flower
                    a weakest flower
          shall be our trust. . . .
          Of asphodel, that greeny flower,
               I come, my sweet,
                    to sing to you!
          My heart rouses
               thinking to bring you news
                    of something
          that concerns you
               and conerns many men. Look at
                    what passes for the new.
          You will not find it there but in
               despised poems.
                    It is difficult
          to get the news from poems
               yet men die miserably every day
                    for lack
          Of what is found there.
```
                              ("Asphodel, That Greeny Flower")

It is the will, man's desire for gardens, that makes a garden out of a place of stone, that "fills up" loneliness, that makes that weakest flower, love, flourish where alienation (silence) can kill. It is poetry, blessed child of the will, that can turn shrieks to lullabies, that makes life an affair of the heart.[7]

No poet has been more subject to metacritical imprecisions, nor has invited through his life and style more random, unfocused comment than Ezra Pound. It will take more than the few summary remarks here—it will take the full critical handling—to persuade the reader as to what ideas are at the center of Pound's enormous lyric and dramatic meditation, *The Cantos*.[8] At that center I find as the controlling idea of the whole one version of the idea of illusion as value, and I want here simply to present enough documentation to outline the argument, to demonstrate again the prevalence of the idea in modern poetry:

          And the wave runs in the beach-groove:
          "Eleanor, . . .

And by the beach-run, Tyro
       Twisted arms of the sea-god,
Lithe sinews of water, gripping her, cross-hold,
And the blue-gray glass of the wave tents them,
Glare azure of water, cold-welter, close cover. . . .

And by Scios,
       to left of the Naxos passage,
Naviform rock overgrown,
       algae cling to its edge,
There is a wine-red glow in the shallows,
       a tin flash in the sun-dazzle.

                                 (Canto 2)

Three events of the imagination are here elliptically linked by the conjunction "and" (as are all events in the canto and, often, in the whole poem). Poets (Pound is saying) look at cold waves and gray color of ocean and populate its flux with personages, of, say, old men murmuring of Helens of Troy and Eleanors of Aquitaine; wave rolling on wave is seen as an embrace of, say, Neptune and Tyro; a wine-red glow in the shallows can conjure up the legend of the wine god, Bacchus:

And by the rock-pool a young boy loggy with vine-must, . . .

God-sleight then, god-sleight:
Beasts like shadows in glass,
       a furred tail upon nothingness.
void air taking pelt.
Lifeless air become sinewed, . . .
       And I worship.
I have seen what I have seen.

The voice is that of a sailor who watched Bacchus turn empty ocean and air into a menagerie. Pound takes the myth from Ovid's *Metamorphoses* and makes it new, makes it his own as one example ("and . . . and") of the poetic imagination's eternally metamorphosing natural process into personal or public myth.

And of a later year,
       pale in the wine-red algae,

If you will lean over the rock,
                    the coral face under wave-tinge,
Rose-paleness under water-shift,
                    Ileuthyeria, fair Dafne of sea-bords,
The swimmer's arms turned to branches,
Who will say in what year,
                    fleeing what band of tritons,
The smooth brows, seen, and half seen,
                    now ivory stillness.

And So-shu churned in the sea, So-shu also,
                    using the long moon for a churn-stick . . .
Lithe turning of water,
                    sinews of Poseidon,
Black azure and hyaline,
                    glass wave over Tyro,
Close cover, unstillness,
                    bright welter of wave-cords. . . .

And we have heard the fauns chiding Proteus
                    in the smell of hay under the olive-trees,
And the frogs singing against the fauns
                    in the half-light.
And . . .

The "you" addressed is the sensitive reader; the "you" becomes the more intimate "we" as the reader is initiated into the
worship of the poetic consciousness of any time or nation
("So-shu also") which transforms in the mind wave-tinge to
rose Ileuthyeria, wave-motion to fleeing tritons, hay-smell and
half-light into fauns. The conjunctions, the linkages of examples can be endless (Protean), for the imagination's deifying
process is endless. Pound says to his soul in an earlier poem

> Will we not find some headland consecrated
> By aery apostles of terrene delight,
> Will not our cult be founded on the waves,
> Clear sapphire, cobalt, cyanine,
> On triune azures, the impalpable
> Mirrors unstill of the eternal change?
>
> ("Blandula, Tenulla, Vagula")

The religious language, especially the trinity of the "triune azures" is carefully poised; the self-delighting imagination creates its own perishable gods, which mirror our desire for gods (the light of reality mirrors but waves' color and motion).

The question Pound asks to open this early poem has a young man's bravura: "What hast thou, O my soul, with paradise?" The older poet sees the full difficulty of man's desire for meaning in a world of "eternal change."

> I don't know how humanity stands it
> > with a painted paradise at the end of it
> without a painted paradise at the end of it
> > > > (Canto 74)

That is, all absolutist mythologies may be illusion, but, at the same time, life without the beauties and values with which mythologies invest reality is unendurable. So that

> > > nothing matters but the quality
> > of the affection—
> > in the end—
> > > > (Canto 76)

Not "truth," not "reality." Each man makes his own heaven (another's hell) out of phenomenological reality:

> What thou lovest well remains,
> > > the rest is dross
> What thou lov'st well shall not be reft from thee
> What thou lov'st well is thy true heritage
> Whose world, or mine or theirs
> > > or is it of none?
> First came the seen, then thus the palpable
> > Elysium, though it were in the halls of hell,
> What thou lovest well is thy true heritage
> > > > (Canto 81)

The position takes its full meaning only in context, but, I would assert, in that context, at the center of meaning in the lines, is the idea of illusion as value, the idea of holding to a core of personal meaning and affection when all things are being "reft from thee." No man's world is the "real," for the mind humanizes and personalizes all the eye sees, and it can— or should—do nothing else. The position is in its own way as bald a statement as that of Stevens which opens this essay, and the two are clearly related. Both are measures of the distance modern culture—as it is seen by these modern poets—has drifted metacritically from the attitudes of preceding centuries.[9]

❧

> O brightest! though too late for antique vows,
>   Too, too late for the fond believing lyre,
> When holy were the haunted forest boughs,
>   Holy the air, the water, and the fire;
> Yet even in these days so far retired
>   From happy pieties, thy lucent fans,
>   Fluttering among the faint Olympians,
> I see, and sing, by my own eyes inspired.
>
> John Keats, "Ode to Psyche"

Anticipations of such modern poetic attitudes are, to be sure, found in the previous century. This is not to say that one might redefine the romanticism of nineteenth-century poetry in terms of the twentieth-century idea, or the twentieth-century idea as, say, a neoromanticism. I intend here only to point briefly to some of the precursors of the modern position outlined above.

Wordsworth's lament in "The World Is Too Much with Us" comes first to mind:

> . . . Great God! I'd rather be
> A Pagan suckled in a creed outworn;
> So might I, standing on this peasant lea,
> Have glimpses that would make me less forlorn;
> Have sight of Proteus rising from the sea;
> Or hear old Triton blow his wreathèd horn.

Illusion preferable to truth—it is the idea, but expressed in an ejaculation of impatience within the full Wordsworthian context of a Christian culture a bit alien and ailing, but available. The idea is also perhaps fleetingly considered in stanza 9 of the "Ode: Intimations of Immortality":

> Those shadowy recollections,
>   Which *be they what they may*,
> Are yet the fountain light of all our day,
> Are yet a master light of all our seeing;
>   Uphold us, cherish, and have power to make
> Our noisy years *seem* moments in the being
> Of the eternal silence.
>
> (Italics mine)

But it is an idea which must wait its time before it becomes a philosophic buttress for the spirit of many modern poets. With respect to Wordsworth it is perhaps in those moving symbolic (unconscious?) extensions of himself, in the solitary, singing reaper, the indomitable leech-gatherer, the Lucy that once made nature alive, that the idea is considered at a deeper psychological level, and where the full implications of Wordsworth's line "By our own spirits are we deified" are obliquely explored.[10]

The case is the same with Coleridge in his "Dejection Ode":

> Ah! from the soul itself must issue forth
> A light, a glory, a fair luminous cloud
>   Enveloping the Earth—
> And from the soul itself must there be sent
>   A sweet and potent voice, of its own birth,
> Of all sweet sounds the life and element!

The question is whether Coleridge is lamenting in this poem a personal loss of imaginative cognizance of a transcendent Higher Reality which invests life with joy and value, or, rather, if the joy and value in life come only from the created fancies of a healthy, simple spirit:

> May all the stars hang bright above her dwelling.
>   Silent as though they watched the sleeping Earth!
>   With light heart may she rise,
>   Gay fancy, cheerful eyes,
>   Joy lift her spirit, joy attune her voice;
> To her may all things live, from pole to pole,
> Their life the eddying of her living soul!

The "as though" can be seen in a modern "as if" context, the eddying of the soul can be seen as the "throwing back," the "backward motion" of the imagination against the stream of reality of Frost's "West-Running Brook." The great bulk of Coleridge's later writing persuades one to read the poem in a romantic-transcendental context. The possibility that Coleridge in an oblique way, as with Wordsworth, at times meditated also (and guiltily) on the sadder modern idea of illusion as value is likely there too. The idea however is not part of the body of central attitudes of either poet.

A heavily dualistic universe is described in Shelley's "Mont Blanc." One has there hints of transcendent meaning behind the veil of the sensuous universe, but also hints of a frightening meaninglessness if there is nothing behind the veil. The poem ends ambiguously, the poet addressing the phenomenological universe figured as Mont Blanc in this way:

> And what were thou, and earth, and stars, and sea,
> If to the human mind's imaginings
> Silence and solitude were vacancy?

That is, silence and solitude *must* be meaningful, the poet's imaginings must have some touch of divinity, or they are but meaningless illusions. The poet's will cannot indulge this latter supposition for long. As with Coleridge and Wordsworth, Shelley moves on towards one sort of transcendent belief (see below, pp. 54–57).

It is in Keats that one finds consistently the more modern stance, a sense of the inadequacy of beauty to quench the thirst for permanence in a world of mutability, and a concomitant sense that beauty is absolutely necessary for life, though not, perhaps, the "truth" about life:

> Away! away! for I will fly to thee
> . . . on the viewless wings of Poesy,
> Though the dull brain perplexes and retards:
> Already with thee! tender is the night. . . .
>
> Forlorn! the very word is like a bell
> To toll me back from thee to my sole self!
> Adieu! the fancy cannot cheat so well
> As she is famed to do, deceiving elf. . . .
>
> ("Ode to a Nightingale")

Beauty, that is, is not truth save within the nightingale's, or the urn's, or the poem's pattern. But no matter, it is the truth while we are in the pattern, and outside that pattern, that context, all is disordered, fleeting, and so, ugly. This sense in Keats of a nontranscendent and temporary solace of the spirit through beauty ("fancy," when it ceases to give solace) is one aspect of the modern tragic tone which readers have found in Keats.

With Poe, the underlying tone is of one for whom even the temporary solace of beauty (what he calls "romance") is hardly available any longer:

> I *have been* happy, though but in a dream.
> I have been happy—and I love the theme:
> Dreams! in their vivid coloring of life,
> As in that fleeting, shadowy, misty strife
> Of semblance with reality which bring
> To the delirious eye, more lovely things
> Of paradise and love. . . .
>
> ("Dreams")

"Romance" is called a "painted paroquet" of youth which can do little to solace the late "condor years." And yet

> . . . when an hour with calmer wings
> Its down upon my spirit flings—

> That little time with lyre and rhyme
> To while away—forbidden things!
> My heart would feel to be a crime
> Unless it trembled with the strings.
>
> ("Romance")

Poe's hours of calm were few, the mindscapes of his poetry project a haunted man, cursed with tortuous anxieties (much like his master, Coleridge). He yearned for the transcendent "Eldorado," praised the illusionary world of dreams, and lived in the nightmarish "ultimate dim Thule."

The euphoric optimism of tone of the Walt Whitman of the early *Song of Myself* would seem to be the antipode of Poe's spiritual condition, the poet having no need for the idea of illusion as value. But the darker side of Whitman—the nightmare visions of "The Sleepers" (published together with *Song of Myself* in 1855), "Out of the Cradle Endlessly Rocking," "As I Ebb'd with the Ocean of Life," "When Lilacs Last," and others in Whitman's later poetry—has been more clearly focused since Stephen Whicher's essay in *The Presence of Walt Whitman* (1962).

> O baffled, balk'd, bent to the very earth
> Oppress'd with myself that I have dared to open my mouth,
> Aware now that amid all that blab whose echoes recoil upon me
>   I have not once had the least idea who I am,
> But that before all my arrogant poems the real Me stands yet
>   untouch'd, untold, altogether unreach'd,
> Withdrawn far, mocking me with mock-congratulatory signs and
>   bows,
> With peals of distant ironical laughter at every word I have
>   written,
> Pointing in silence to these songs, and then to the sand beneath.
>
> ("As I Ebb'd with the Ocean of Life")

It is in this mood, of Whitman's "many moods, one contradicting another," that we can read a late poem of Whitman's in the context of the idea of illusion as value:

A noiseless patient spider,
I mark'd where on a little promontory it stood isolated,
Mark'd how to explore the vacant vast surrounding,
It launch'd forth filament, filament, filament out of itself,
Ever unreeling them, ever tirelessly speeding them.

And you O my soul where you stand,
Surrounded, detached, in measureless oceans of space,
Ceaselessly musing, venturing, throwing, seeking the spheres to
    connect them,
Till the bridge you will need be form'd, till the ductile anchor
    hold,
Till the gossamer thread you fling catch somewhere,
    O my soul.

("A Noiseless Patient Spider")

Out of oneself one forms in the vacancy, the void, the bridge (of gossamer thread) that one needs, a bridge that makes some connections somewhere, anywhere. One weaves mythologies out of one's need to make meaning out of vacancy and isolation. It looks like the modern desperate situation—Stevens's condition of poverty; it certainly is not the euphoric posture dominant in *Song of Myself*.

But there is that Whitman of other moods, among which is the Emersonian transcendentalist of the standard textbooks (see below, pp. 57–62). Whitman has not the stability of posture, of outlook, toward poetry as blessed fiction that characterizes the modern poets we have discussed. Whitman, as do the other nineteenth-century poets mentioned, touches only occasionally on the idea of illusion as value, the poetical idea that has been a dominant, yet submerged, precise yet obscured idea of modern art. It is the idea that has made imprecise the explication of many modern poetical texts seen through a romantic, transcendental, or other metacritical focus. It is the idea which to a large extent, in the opinion of this reader, makes modern poetry modern.

All metaphysics perhaps is poetry, but Platonic metaphysics is good poetry. . . . (George Santayana—"Shelley" in *Winds of Doctrine*, p. 180).

If, as Santayana asserts, the fundamental axioms of all metaphysical systems are unprovable (and this is a dominant philosophic position of modern times), then what makes one metaphysics better than another? The question is reduced by Santayana to: What makes one poetry better than another? which is an aesthetic question. The modern poets we have discussed above start from the same premise as Santayana and they would respond to the question, as Santayana would seem to in the Shelley essay, by saying that it is not "truth" that matters so much in life and art, as the quality of a man's imagination. Or as Pound puts it, "nothing matters but the quality of the affection." The position implies some attitudes which would flow in an emotional logic. I want to try to outline, to give what seems to me a précis, of those corollary attitudes and a sense of their importance to the modern cultural situation.

> It was when I said,
> "There is no such thing as the truth,"
> That the grapes seemed fatter.
> The fox ran out of his hole.
>
> (Stevens, "On the Road Home")

"Truth," whether it be the scientist's or the sociologist's or the psychologist's truth, rests ultimately on metaphysical hypotheses to which we are under no obligation to assent and which may or may not be productive of any beauty at all. Beauty, Stevens and the poets of this persuasion would say, is in order and fulfillment. If "truth" of any sort be productive of little or no beauty, then we are under no obligation to worship such "reality," rather under an obligation to ourselves and to human need to select from life, to order life into patterns which make it acceptable (see chapter 7 for the fuller development of these positions).

One must respect, these poets would say, another man's

loves (it implies the same treatment of one's own loves), but one must reject all absolutisms. To the skeptical eye of these poets and of most poets, there is no personal or collective millennium, political, social, spiritual, or otherwise, to come on this side of the grave:

> What is the city over the mountains
> Cracks and reforms and bursts in the violet air
> Falling towers
> Jerusalem Athens Alexandria
> Vienna London
> Unreal
>
> (T. S. Eliot, *The Waste Land*, sec. 5)

And absolutisms and arrogancies can dry up the beauties one *can* attain:

> My mind, because the minds that I have loved,
> The sort of beauty that I have approved,
> Prosper but little, has dried up of late,
> Yet knows that to be choked with hate
> My well be of all evil chances chief. . . .
> An intellectual hatred is the worst. . . .
> . . . arrogance and hatred are the wares
> Peddled in the thoroughfares.
>
> (Yeats, "A Prayer for My Daughter")

It would be the thrust of these poets that it is the opposite of arrogance that needs to be cultivated as an attitude for the twentieth-century spiritual condition: if not humility exactly, then sympathy—a feeling for man's hunger for value, meaning, continuity. The attitude toward life and art counseled by the poetry we have been examining is of a wider love for orders, continuities, contexts of value whose postulates may be illusionary but which are nonetheless lovely and necessary. It is an attitude without political program, without dogma, a tendency only, a spirit sad, weak, and human, one which understands man's love of order and blesses when it sees pattern, which will praise loyalty to ideals not one's own and respect continuities outside one's own loved context.

"Cultures" are social contexts. Hart Crane's *The Bridge* is in part a celebration of the mythologies that impelled cultural contexts of the past, and a lament for the largely de-mythologized twentieth century American cultural context. So that some cultures, some contexts, are better than others. We are back to the implied question of the epigraph from Santayana: What constitutes a better culture, or better poetry, or a better metaphysic? It would seem that we should judge according to how well and deeply a given context (cultural or poetical) recognizes (1) a fundamental, irreducible tragedy in man's experience of life; (2) a fundamental, irreducible desire in man for permanence, belief, and value; (3) a fundamental, irreducible need in man for ideas, myths, assumptions, illusions, what you will, to satisfy these desires, no matter how transiently. These recognitions must be part of a context poets such as these can accept. The depth and quality, coherence and continuity of such recognition is an internal intrinsic judgment to be made within a context. Outside a context may well be the frightening void of meaninglessness. Inside a context however can be, to be sure, almost as insufferable—for the outsider—as the void, if it is based on arrogance, dogmatism, absolute categories of any sort of group-think, if it will tolerate no mythologies but its own.

The culture, the poem, the embracing metaphysic must have, then, sentiment, tolerance, pity for the irreducible tragedy in human life, and empathy for the imagination's children of desire. To be human is to desire and so to love and to believe, illusion or no. It is this tone only that these poets project: a spirit, attitude, that has hardly anywhere else to go if it is to be human. And in this modern situation it may prove to be a tonality that can outsurvive all sorts of (see Marianne Moore) modern steamrollers.

Notes

1. "An Ordinary Evening in New Haven," sec. 5, lines 1–2.
2. "Esthetique du Mal" sec. 11, lines 10–11.

3. See my *Wallace Stevens: An Anatomy of Figuration* (Philadelphia, 1965) for an extended exposition of this position.

4. See my *The Rape of Cinderella* (Bloomington, Ind., 1970), chapters on *The Bridge* and its critics, for a fuller treatment.

5. See "Two Songs from a Play" and "Among School Children."

6. For a reading of "Lapis Lazuli" and of Yeats's poetry and poetics in general from a position close to mine, see Frank Lentricchia's *The Gaiety of Language* (Berkeley, Calif., 1968).

7. We have been speaking of Williams, but it sounds much like Stevens. Which ought to remind us: an essay like this on the currency of an idea among poets in the modern situation is but a halfway house for criticism. The poets here discussed are major artists of our time who have often been badly served by imprecise metacriticism masking as criticism (the Williams above is central Williams, but to many will be an unfamiliar Williams). To focus as this essay does on an idea central to the tonality of each of the poets is but to approach closer to the full critical operation: the precise probing of the unique and complex body of attitudes in the work of the individual poet.

8. See my *The Cantos of Ezra Pound: The Lyric Mode* (Baltimore, Md., 1975).

9. The modern idea here treated is there in places in poets as widely disparate as John Crowe Ransom, e. e. Cummings, Lawrence Ferlinghetti, and other poets, there in Henry James, Ernest Hemingway, and other novelists—part, really, of the cultural air we breathe.

10. See Wordsworth's "Resolution and Independence."

3
On the Posture of Exultant Dualism

The poets I touch upon in this essay are as diverse as human beings are diverse, but have in common that they all slip at times into the posture, the pretense really, of having exhaled the contraries of existence into some sort of cosmic Unity while in reality succeeding only in dramatizing or avoiding them. The concomitant tone of arrogance, and the inadequacy in analysis and dramatization which at times blemishes the work of these poets is a manifestation of the "categorical" cast of mind, the penchant in the mind for the organizing of systems, archetypes, topologies, paradigms, that are not answers, but only new groupings, pigeonholings, pretending to be answers.

I have written earlier and briefly on this cast of mind (*The Rape of Cinderella*, pp. 220–28). But the matter had already received brilliant, albeit elliptical, treatment in Professor William Wimsatt's *Hateful Contraries* (1965), especially in the opening and concluding chapters. Wimsatt's terms for the mental posture of which I am speaking are "manichean," "promethean" and "the easy celebration of the eternal Orc." The final allusion is of course to William Blake, and it is to Blake that I want first to turn:

> Without Contraries is no progression. Attrraction and Repulsion, Reason and Energy, Love and Hate, are necessary to Human existence.
> From these contraries spring what the religious call Good & Evil. Good is the passive that obeys Reason. Evil is the active springing from Energy. (*The Marriage of Heaven and Hell*)

The lines of course, especially the last, are intended to be provocative, paradoxical. They are intended to expose the smugness, the limitations of the thinking of the "religious" on what is good and what is evil. Even more provoking and, again, consciously so is the "Sooner murder an infant in its cradle than nurse unacted desires" later in the poem. Blake is saying "It is your world, you religious hypocrites, that has created a society where such outrageous choices can be forced upon one." "But," other poets might say, "What of fundamental, irreducible Evil? not the Evil in systems, but the uneradicable Evil in individual men?" The question cannot be addressed at the level of abstraction from which Blake has chosen to speak.

No poet of genius has dramatized tragic, dualistic contraries within the individual soul better than Blake in his *Songs of Innocence and Experience*. The poise, the tact, the balanced equilibrium of most of that volume is, however, submerged in *The Marriage of Heaven and Hell* and the later works by a desire to preach a system with much of the pat smugness of religious zeal, creating a tonality which cannot hide the minimalness of what the system has to offer the individual soul:

> . . . All deities reside in the human breast. . . .
> . . . God only Acts & Is, in existing beings or Men. . . .
> The worship of God is: Honouring his gifts in other men, each according to his genius, and loving the greatest men best: those who envy or caluminate great men hate God; for there is no other God. *(The Marriage of Heaven and Hell)*

> And it is thus Created. Lo, the Eternal Great Humanity,
> To whom be Glory & Dominion Evermore, Amen . . .
> "Whatever can be Created can be Annihilated: Forms cannot:
> The Oak is cut down by the Ax, the Lamb falls by the Knife,
> But their Forms Eternal Exist For-ever. Amen.
>   Hallelujah!"
>   (*Milton*, Sec's. 33, 35)
> "Go, tell them that the Worship of God is honouring his gifts
> In other men & loving the greatest men best, each according
> To his Genius which is the Holy Ghost in Man; there is no
>   other

God than that God who is the intellectual fountain of
 Humanity. . . ."

           . . . & Albion knew
 that it
Was the Lord, the Universal Humanity; & Albion saw his Form
A Man, & they conversed as Man with Man in Ages of Eternity.
And the Divine Appearance was the likeness & similitude of
 Los.

           (*Jerusalem*, Sec's. 91, 96)

The position outlined here is paradigmatic for the cast of mind
I am attempting to delineate, and manifests itself in a humanism which, without a God external to men, exalts as "Divine"
the creative achievements and potential in "Man" taken as an
abstract entity, focuses on permanent Forms and states of
consciousness, not the perishing consciousness of individual
men. The position pitches its camp at a high bivouac, beyond
the 'sufferings in the abyss' of men who do not have much
Poetic Genius and who do not want to die, who cannot be
satisfied by appeals to the self-sufficiency of psychic moments
or to other's achievements, past or future. In Blake's system,
Albion represents the integrated mind; Urizen and Orc the
reason and energy of the fragmented mind; Los the poetic
imagination that can reintegrate the mind of Man, and restore
Albion to his prelapsarian mental paradise. Thus the
categorizing, organizing, schematizing mind creates mental
allegories of a humanism of the sort Wallace Stevens in
"Crude Foyer" calls "Humanity's bleak crown." The "Hal-
lelujah" in the passage from *Milton* is intended as a satiric
thrust against misguided zeal, but its use in propagating
Blake's true gospel of humanity creates a grim ironic distance
between the exulting rhetoric and the flintiness of the position. The discontinuity of tone resultant from the promise of
the rhetoric and the contrasting meagerness in the position for
the individual human soul is characteristic of much of Blake
and much of the poetry which this essay examines.

Shelley's allegory of the fragmented mind, *Prometheus Un-*

bound, revolves around a similar humanism and a similar millennial dream dreamt about the same abstract entity, "Man":

> . . .Thought's stagnant chaos, unremoved for ever,
> Till hate, and fear, and pain, light-vanquished shadows,
>   fleeing,
>
> Leave Man. . . .
>
> Man, Oh, not men! a chain of linkèd thought,
> Of love and might to be divided not. . . .
>
> Man, one harmonious soul of many a soul,
> Whose nature is its own divine control. . . .
>
> Labour, and pain, and grief, in life's green grove
> Sport like tame beasts, none knew how gentle they
>   could be!
>
> His will, wilth all mean passions, bad delights,
>   And selfish cares, its trembling satellites,
> A spirit ill to guide, but mighty to obey,
>   Is as a tempest-winged ship, whose helm
>   Love rules. . . .
>
> ("Earth's Song," act 4)

This (1818–19) is the high-water mark of Shelley's idealistic
humanism which hovers now about Platonism, now over the
ground of materialism. Shelley had begun as a necessitarian
and atheist—see the early essays "Necessity," "On Miracles,"
and "On a Future State," postulated on the idea that all life is
but chemical combination. In the last lines of "Mt. Blanc"
(1816, see above p. 44) Shelley wavers between a materialistic and a Platonistic world view (cf. the same wavering in
the more platonically oriented "Hymn to Intellectual Beauty"
of the same year). The passage from *Prometheus Unbound* above
is heavily Platonistic in appearance but, as with Blake, attempts to do without an external "Power" or "One" which
draws the individual soul from hate to love, attempting to
make do with the dubious idea that the chemical soul is its *own*

divine control, and that hate, fear, pain, labor, and grief are somehow eradicable, mere "shadows." This all, it seems to me, is a mere papering over of the contraries with the rhetoric of exultant dualism. As Simone Weil has pointed out, scientific materialism ("force" is her term) and humanism make strange bedfellows:

> The philosophy which has inspired the laical spirit and political radicalism is founded at the same time on this science and on this humanism, which are, as can be seen, manifestly incompatible with each other. . . .
>
> During the course of the last few centuries, the contradiction between science and humanism has been felt confusedly, although the intellectual courage has always been lacking to look it squarely in the face. . . .
> Force is not a machine for automatically creating justice. It is a blind mechanism, which produces indiscriminately and impartially just or unjust results, but, by all the laws of probability, nearly always unjust ones.
> Where force is absolutely sovereign, justice is absolutely unreal. (*The Need for Roots,* pp. 241–43)

Shelley's scientific materialism waned, his Platonism grew, as he approached the time of his early death:

> . . . but the pure spirit shall flow
> Back to the burning fountain whence it came,
> A portion of the Eternal
> . . . the one Spirit's plastic stress
> Sweeps through the dull dense world
> . . . that Power . . .
> Which wields the world with never-wearied love,
> Sustains it from beneath, and kindles it above. . . .
> That Light whose smile kindles the Universe,
> That Beauty in which all things work and move,
> That Benediction which the eclipsing Curse
> Of birth can quench not. . . .
>
> ("Adonais," sec. 38, 42, 43, 54)

But, as the "curse of birth" expression indicates, so too waned the humanism and the political radicalism. The world came to seem much more intractable and its evil more fundamental than they had earlier seemed. "Adonais" and "The Triumph of Life" are deeply permeated with a disillusion concerning the perfectibility of man and society. The vision of existence in "Adonais" is of "corpses in a charnel." Shelley wishes for death to avoid the "world's bitter wind," the "contagion of the world's slow stain" (cf. the "ghastly dance" about "life's chariot" in "The Triumph of Life"). The contraries are not to be resolved on earth:

> 'Tis we, who lost in stormy visions keep
> With phantoms an unprofitable strife,
> And in a mad trance, strike with our spirit's knife
> Invulnerable nothings. . . .
>
> ("Adonais" sec. 39)

Shelley shadowboxed with phantoms in *Prometheus Unbound* trying to reconcile an idealistic humanism with his acute sense of man's past inhumanity to man. But the vision of *Prometheus Unbound* hardly convinces, never overcomes what is in fact the irresolution in the artist between his exulting in man's potential and his awareness of the prevalent baseness of his mind and acts. The characters of *Prometheus Unbound*, Demogorgon, Ocean, Asia, and so on, are all fragments of this divided mind, though the rhetoric tries to have one think the author stands in a posture of certainty. We often sense the irresolution beneath the desired wisdom in Shelley, but tragically in some of the last poems, particularly "Adonais" and "Triumph of Life," Shelley achieves for himself a continuity of attitude and strength of position by turning his back on life, by separating his idealism from his humanism, by postulating a Platonic Unity elsewhere than on this materialistic, dualistic earth.

Walt Whitman, too, underwent a period of disillusion after the buoyant state of consciousness depicted in the "Song of Myself," a disillusion traced through the poems by Stephen Whicher (see above pp. 46–47) and only partially obscured in the later reworkings of the full *Leaves of Grass*. Whitman's first edition of *Leaves of Grass* (1855) contains what was to become

"Song of Myself," and eleven other short poems, including "The Sleepers," which is something like the reverse of the euphoric consciousness of "Song of Myself." The 1855 volume attempts in places to minimize, as Blake and Shelley had attempted to do, the profundity, the ineluctability of evil and tragedy:

> Showing the best and dividing it from the worst,
>   age vexes age,
> Knowing the perfect fitness and equanimity of
>   things, while they discuss I am silent,
>   and go bathe and admire myself. . . .
>   ("Song of Myself," sec. 3)
> What is called good is perfect, and what is called
>   sin is just as perfect, ...
>   ("To Think of Time," sec. 8)

The Walt Whitman of the 1855 volume often expands himself into a presence embracing all of experience, an eye which in its moments confidently sees through death and pain and the sordid anguishes of life to a transcendent unity:

> O I Perceive after all so many uttering tongues
> And I perceive they do not come from the roofs of mouths for
>   nothing.
> I wish I could translate the hints about the dead young men and
>   women,
> And the hints about old men and mothers, and the offspring
>   taken soon out of their laps.
> What do you think has become of the women and children?
>
> They are alive and well somewhere . . .
> And to die is different from what any one supposed, and luckier.
>   ("Song of Myself," sec. 6)
> Do you suspect death? If I were to suspect death I should die
>   now,
> Do you think I could walk pleasantly and well-suited toward
>   annihilation?
>
> Pleasantly and well-suited I walk, ...
>   ("To Think of Time," sec. 8)

But despite such bootstrap assertions of an exultant metaphysic, what is constantly *rendered* in dramatic vignettes are endless details of the contingent world, an enormous wealth of particulars of a heavily dualistic experience of life:

> The little one sleeps in its cradle,
> I lift the gauze and look a long time, and silently brush away
> flies with my hand. . . .
> The suicide sprawls on the bloody floor of the bedroom,
> I witness the corpse with its dabbled hair, I note where the
> pistol has fallen. . . .
> The lunatic is carried at last to the asylum a confirmed case,
> He will never sleep any more as he did in the cot in his mother's
> bedroom;
> The jour printer with gray head and gaunt jaws works at his
> case,
> He turns his quid of tobacco, his eyes get blurred with the
> manuscript;
> The malformed limbs are tied to the anatomist's table,
> What is removed drops horribly in a pail. . . .
> Arrests of criminals, slights, adulterous offers made,
> acceptances, reflections with convex lips,
> I mind them or the show or resonance of them—I come and I
> depart.
>
> ("Song of Myself," sec. 8, 15)

The following passage unconvincingly asserts that everything that happens is good and acceptable, including the implications of the doctrines of materialism and positive science:

> Here or henceforward it is all the same to me,
>   I accept Time absolutely.
> It alone is without flaw, it alone rounds and completes all.
> That mystic baffling wonder alone completes all.
> I accept Reality and dare not question it,
> Materialism first and last imbuing.
> Hurrah for positive science! long live exact demonstration!
>
> ("Song of Myself," sec. 23)

This is the bravado of exultant dualism, done partly for the pleasure of paradox, partly, it seems to me, to convince the poet himself. By immense exuberance in the response to all of life, Whitman would have us feel that there is plenty of life left over to take care of death:

> I know I am deathless,
> I know this orbit of mine cannot be swept
>   by a carpenter's compass,
> I know I shall not pass like a child's carlacue
>   cut with a burnt stick at night.
>
> ("Song of Myself," sec. 20)

Consistently in the poem paticulars of the contingent world, like the child's carlacue and the burnt stick at night, so capture our imagination that our emotions tell us that Whitman fears that we *do* pass like the burnt-out stick. Details of the evanescent joy and pain of local scenes and moods so brilliantly caught work against the flat assertions of certitude, in one's mystic moments, in a sort of immortality. The *hunger* for the immortality of evanescent joy is more what "Song of Myself" actually projects.

There is fundamental irresolution in the Whitman of "Song of Myself," the exulting rhetoric hiding at times the poet's deeper intuition that the moments of psychic uplift, or heightened awareness, or cosmic consciousness, while obviously worth the having, change nothing about man's tragic situation, once out of the moment. Only a faith in a personal immortality can do that with any permanence; and so the half-hearted, unconvincing passes at incorporating such a faith in "Song of Myself."

The following is Richard Chase on the blurring of the dualistic vision in Whitman:

> What finally happens is that Whitman loses his sense that his metaphor of self vs. en-masse is a paradox, that self and en-masse are in dialectic opposition. When this sense is lost the spontaneously eventful, flowing, and largely indeterminate universe of "Song of Myself" is replaced by a universe that is both mechanical and vaguely abstract.
>
> (*Walt Whitman Reconsidered*, p. 67)

The paradox, the opposition, of which Chase is speaking is that while the "life-force" in "Man" as an abstraction may be upward and onward, the perishing individual man can hardly be expected to take any great interest in its progress.

Karl Shapiro had apparently and at one time an even lower opinion of Whitman as a thinker than Chase, as witness the following remarks in an essay on Hart Crane's *The Bridge:*

> . . . Walt Whitman presented him with the false vision of life which eventually Crane was to employ for his own self-destruction. . . .
>
> *(Poets at Work*, p. 111)

Several years later Shapiro apparently has had a change of heart:

> He [Whitman] is the one mystical writer of any consequence America has produced; the most original religious thinker we have; the poet of the greatest achievement; the first profound innovator; the most accomplished artist as well. . . .
>
> *(Start with the Sun*, p. 60)

What I want to point out in these quotations is the essentially metacritical foundations for Shapiro's change of opinion. Shapiro, early or late, can, as well as could Randall Jarrell, appreciate a master of poetic lines; what has changed is Shapiro's attitude toward a body of ideas he calls in his essays "cosmic consciousness." It is a set of attitudes that I find often involved in the discontinuities, imprecisions, and arrogancies of posture which this essay attempts to outline. *Start with the Sun* (a collaborative volume) incidentally is typical of what has become a large critical and metacritical movement, the burden of Wimsatt's book. The culture heroes of *Start with the Sun* are Blake, Whitman, Lawrence, Hart Crane, and Dylan Thomas. It is worth remarking that except for Crane these are the very artists that have struck me as both major and flawed, hurt at times by rant to cover irresolution. (I have attempted to demonstrate in my *The Rape of Cinderella*, chapters 12 and 13, that Crane's terrible irresolution as a person did not prevent him from writing a great poem, *The Bridge*, continuous in all its parts. For Lawrence, see the following chapter.)

Dylan Thomas's "And Death Shall Have No Dominion" can stand, I think, as archetypal of the fraudulent tone endemic in the posture of exultant dualism, the dependence on abstract categories and the cultivation of a deceptive rhetoric. The lines boom with affirmations of triumph, of promises to the human spirit concerning Unity and ultimate solace for the terrors of annihilation. The lines *seem* to say that, but the posture of strength and certitude rests on a vision of a unity so abstract, so obliterative of the individual human spirit, the personal ego, that it could make no difference to the wretched if it were the blackest nihilism. "Though lovers be lost love shall not"; "Heads of the characters hammer through daisies": these are the concepts on which the posture of certitude rests. We must deal with a pun on "character" which is finally unconscionable. Diametrically opposite statements are made by the word as it can refer to both man as a type and to the personal idiosyncrasies of specific men. The poem is really speaking about man as a type, but the diction invites the reader to think it is about himself and his personal love. The lines finally say that the type will endure and so will love as a force, though we as personalities will not (see Blake's "Eternal Great Humanity Divine," above). This is hardly an affirmation that can support the bravado that surrounds it. There is nothing wrong with the dualistic vision that essentially underlies the poem—love and death as equally eternal and constantly perishing—but the exultant rhetoric constantly lies about the sadness, the minimalness, of what is being said. Only by understanding the paradoxical lines consistently in that aspect the rhetoric is trying to hide does one come to know the Thomas of this poem, who impresses here as a rather tortured, suffering spirit behind a booming voice.

Much the same could be said about "A Refusal to Mourn the Death, by Fire, of a Child in London." The poet will not mourn, the audience is told, because death is the law of life, is but part of the Process; we all go down into the dark and nature does not mourn: such is mankind's lot. Thomas depends on "mankind" here, as he depends on "love" and "character" in "And Death Shall Have No Dominion," as an abstraction to keep the pain of the personal, the girl's actual death, his death to come, at arm's length.

Thomas is much greater, and more coherent tonally, when, in his more usual context, he simply describes dualistic experience with tortured acuity:

> The force that through the green fuse drives the flower
> Drives my green age; that blasts the roots of trees
> Is my destroyer.
> And I am dumb to tell the crooked rose
> My youth is bent by the same wintry fever.

This, it seems to me, is the true Thomas tonality. The false note creeps in later in the poem:

> The lips of time leech to the fountain head;
> Love drips and gathers, but the fallen blood
> Shall calm her sores.

That is, the sores of love, the fountainhead, will be calmed, though none of the lovers will. This is the Thomas of the pose of equanimity with the process and with death.

The truer Thomas is attuned to the tragic pathos of personal death, no matter how good and fitting Death may be in the abstract:

> And you, my father, there on the sad height,
> Curse, bless, me now with your fierce tears, I pray.
> Do not go gentle into that good night.
> Rage, rage against the dying of the light.

This is the greater Thomas. It is only human to rage against one's personal death, and empathy for this rage is a true humanism, not the humanism that would exult in the "Great Man" or "Great Society" to come. One must rage against the personal, the present contextual indignity, meanness, or evil, not abstract these into a system where the "contraries are necessary to Human existence" and "Evil is the active springing from Energy." It may be that evil exists for an ultimate good, but we do not therefore put the Devil on a throne. At its best the position of exultant dualism merely clothes irresolution with the appearance of optimism or certitude and results in an artistic discontinuity of tone. At its worst it can serve as the base for all sorts of absolutist arrogance and group-think, adoration of process, the callousness to individual evils, etc. Samuel Johnson admirably raged against the posture as it appears in Pope's *Essay on Man* ("Whatever is, is right") in the *Soame Jenyns* review:

> When this author presumes to speak of the universe, I would advise him a little to distrust his own faculties, however large and comprehensive. . . .
> Where has this enquirer added to the little knowledge that we had before? He has told us of the benefits of evil, which no man feels, and relations between distant parts of [the] universe, which he cannot himself conceive. There was enough in this question inconceivable before, and we have little advantage from a new inconceivable solution.
> I do not mean to reproach this author for not knowing what is equally hidden from learning and from ignorance. The shame is to impose words for ideas upon ourselves or others. To imagine that we are going forward when we are only turning round.

Now Yeats saw the world dualistically and he never lost the tact (in his poetry) to present his reconciliations as but partial, insufficient answers. He *will* escape to Innisfree, he *will* be a wild, wicked old man, he *would* be a golden bird upon a bough—the torment involved in these compulsive cries of the will is clear in the poems, as is the realization that these answers will not do, that the poet *is* caught in the "fury and mire of human veins." This is a true humanistic note, the tonality which is lacking in the exultant response to dualistic experience.

4
Stylistic Discontinuity in D. H. Lawrence's *The Rainbow*

And always the light of the transfiguration burned on in their hearts. He went his way, as before, she went her way, to the rest of the world there seemed no change. But to the two of them, there was the perpetual wonder of transfiguration. . . .

He was the sensual male seeking his pleasure, she was the female ready to take hers: but in her own way. A man could turn into a free lance: so then could a woman. She adhered as little as he to the moral world. All that had gone before was nothing to her. She was another woman, under the instance of a strange man. He was a stranger to her, seeking his own ends. Very good. She wanted to see what this stranger would do now, what he was. (D. H. Lawrence, *The Rainbow*, pp. 91, 232)

With Lawrence on a given page everything seems to be certain, final, absolute; the usual words are "always," and "perpetual" for actions which are "unalterable" and "transfiguring" (as in the first passage above). And yet from page *to* page, the characters' emotions flip and flop, those who love unalterably hate their lovers off and on (as in the second passage); those who have attained perpetual transfiguration seem to endure the state in perpetual agony. It is hard to tell wherein those who have the right (Lawrencian) slant on life are happier than those who do not (except for those passages where Lawrence tells us it is so). What the prose consistently says it is giving the reader is a comprehensive ethical (how to live, what to do) system of some absoluteness; what is *rendered* by the prose however, I would say, is rather a close tracing of the turbulent ebb and flow (now ecstatic, now despairing) of the affective life. This latter sensitivity to the constant instability of the emotions in all the personages in the book continually belies the absolutist language (and implied dialectic) constantly proffered. The skeptical reader finds the running discrepancies between the sad and ambiguous human dramas and the exultant, absolutist rhetoric discontinuous here, as he found the similar effect in the poets of the previous chapter.

It is the common procedure in Lawrence discussion as I see it to argue metacritically the value of Lawrence's ethical attitudes and postures before the proper critical questions are asked as to whether Lawrence's style is answerable to the primary critical "law" of coherence or continuity. It will be the burden of this essay that, despite the absoluteness with which attitudes are constantly expressed in *The Rainbow*, the various attitudes struck in the book do not cohere, and that the various styles used to impel the various attitudes constantly clash.

The kinds of questions that ought to be asked about the book are these: (1) Are the characters in the book intended to be uniquely themselves or archetypal (the apocalyptic prose of the first passage above vs. the naturalistic prose of the second). (2) What is the "voice" of the novel? Is it Lawrence's? And if so, always? Is he not sometimes (again consider the passages above) merely paraphrasing what is passing in the mind of his characters? And if so, when, and with how much (if any) irony toward the character? (3) Is there any intent in the novel to create tragic ironies between ideals considered typically Lawrencian—the "Rainbow" condition—and the possibility of achieving them? Or is the book soberly intended as prophecy?

It is time to look at the text. The first pages in their biblical idiom win our sympathies over to the Brangwen men rather completely. The ingathering prose implies that the men are fulfilling their peasant (Abrahamic) destiny and that no more could be asked of them or of life. The men are mythic in their largeness and wholeness; the Brangwen woman seems wrong in her wish for another form of life ("she faced outward to where men moved dominant and creative, having turned their back on the pulsing heat of creation"). So overpowering is the lyricism in the evocation of the simple peasant life that preaching of other deeper, wider, lives later in the book does not convince. He ought not to have created the serene world of his golden age so well if he wished to be "realistic" about that age later. It is not enough to say that Lawrence's ultimate view is complex; the biblical style here and elsewhere is simply too engaging. When we read of "the woman's" admiration and awe of the vicar ("what was it in the vicar, that raised him above common men as man is raised above the beast?"), the prose has made us feel that the woman's judgment is misguided. There is, then, the impression of an Adamic fall from grace when in chapter 2 social upheaval turns the Brangwen men's vision outward toward the great world.

Chapter 2 begins as if we are to have a novel of a society in flux and turmoil, but the chapter settles down, as does most of the book, to an inner analysis of personal problems, spiritual and sexual, first of Tom and Lydia, later of Will and Anna, and finally of Ursula Brangwen. Every so often, however, Lawrence's sensitivity to social problems dominates pages of the book and causes jarring switches in narrative perspective and style. The long sections in the last half of the novel dealing with Ursula's attempt to cope with modern employment and education are cut from a different piece of cloth stylistically than are those of her affair with Skrebensky (or those in the lyrical style of her self-realization in solitude). The rapid surface narrative of the school sections does not harmonize tonally with the intensity, the overwhelming earnestness, of the passages of the inner life. Their juxtapositioning is often humorous in a novel whose radical humorlessness cannot bear to be exposed:

So they stood in the utter, dark kiss, that triumphed over them both, subjected them, knitted them into one fecund nucleus of the fluid darkness.
It was bliss, it was the nucleolating of the fecund darkness. Once the vessel had vibrated till it was shattered, the light of

consciousness gone, then the darkness reigned, and the unutterable satisfaction. . . .

Mr. Brunt was crouching at the small stove, putting a little rice-pudding into the oven. He rose then, and attentively poked in a small saucepan on the hob with a fork. Then he replaced the saucepan lid.

"Aren't they done?" asked Ursula gaily, breaking in on his tense absorption.

She always kept a bright, blithe manner, and was pleasant to all the teachers. For she felt like a swan among the geese, of superior heritage and belonging. And her pride at being the swan in this ugly school was not yet abated.

"Not yet," replied Mr. Brunt, laconic.

"I wonder if my dish is hot," she said, bending down at the oven. She half expected him to look for her, but he took no notice. She was hungry and she poked her finger eagerly in the pot to see if her brussels sprouts and potatoes and meat were ready. They were not. (Pp. 447, 378)

There are perhaps four broad styles operative in the book, none of which sets well with the others: (1) the "biblical-lyrical," as in the first chapter and the end of chapter 3, where all is rhythmical, serene, inevitable, the assumption is made that we all understand the pattern beneath, and great causative links are implied; (2) the rapid surface narrative, the naturalistic handling of the exterior life, locale, and local manners; (3) the "nucleotic," expressive, frantic, pulsating, apocalyptic, as in the first of the two passages immediately above; (4) the symbolic, as with the cathedral, the rainbow, and the rushing moon and patchy cloud that end chapter 1. The effect of switches from style to style often gives the impression of improvisation, of variation without much progress. The cathedral symbol, for instance, of chapter 7, focuses much in the Lawrencian vision and is valuable for that. The chapter is much less valuable in progressing the narrative, as Anna's fight against her husband's impulse toward religious dogma has already been waged and won in the preceding chapter. In the cathedral chapter the battle is for no convincing reason refought and rewon in a different style. This is typical of the curious movement of the book, the seeming purposefulness and assurance of its rhetorics as to where it is going while the various styles seem in fact to be riding emotional flows of the author whither they go. (Lawrence tells us that *The Rainbow* is the product of eight separate drafts, and I think it is quite likely that much of the discontinuity and disjointedness one feels in the book is the result of imperfect welding of different sections of draft copy.)[1]

Lawrence does not discriminate well between contingent and significant emotion. The prose renders all emotion as equally important, serious, and meaningful. Hence the impression that all the characters are faceless walking Ids. There is no question that Lawrence feels he is constantly probing deep into human personality, but we are at liberty to disagree, to feel that he is most often dealing with contingent emotion as if it were inexpressibly illuminating. Is the following profound in its knowledge, or simple acute in its tracing of vagaries of emotion?

> He was glad to leave school. It had not been unpleasant, he had enjoyed the companionship of the other youths, or had thought he enjoyed it, the time had passed very quickly, in endless activity. But he knew all the time that he was in an ignominious position, in this place of learning. He was aware of failure all the while, of incapacity. But he was too healthy and sanguine to be wretched, he was too much alive. Yet his soul was wretched almost to hopelessness. (P. 12)

He was glad to leave school, although it had not been unpleasant. He *had* enjoyed (Lawrence speaking, or Tom?); he *thought* he had enjoyed it (again Lawrence's ex cathedra statement or Tom's hindsight of a later time than the first clause of the sentence?). "But he *knew all the time* . . ."; the question occurs, why did not this sort of intuitive knowledge extend to his knowing whether he had enjoyed it or not? Apparently with the last two sentences of the passage it is implied that consciously he was *not* wretched, unconsciously he *was*, though it is not clear, again, if Tom comes to know this in hindsight or if Lawrence is telling us of emotions which the limited Tom

Brangwen could never articulate, even to himself. The vocabulary is full of absolutes; Lawrence seems to be preaching through paradox of contraries beyond our ken.

Another example: one wonders how much the wiser we are about Anna from this sort of description through contradictions:

> The girl was at once shy and wild. She had a curious contempt for ordinary people, a benevolent superiority. She was very shy, and tortured with misery when people did not like her. On the other hand, she cared very little for anybody save her mother, whom she still rather resentfully worshipped, and her father, whom she loved and patronized, but upon whom she depended.(P. 93)

This sense of the instability of human character in Lawrence comes presumably from an uncompromising honesty to the confusion of the affective life as he feels it. The trouble is his equally intense desire for absolutes—for the biblical substance as well as style.

Chapter 2—"They Live at the Marsh"—contains early an exquisite section on the hesitancy of the lovers Tom and Lydia, their "openings" and "closings" to one another coming (perhaps inevitably) out of step. It is in the nature of a tour de force—these hesitations are not really very important, with or without them Tom and Lydia are sure to come together. Or so Lawrence tells us in his biblical-lyrical idiom. The diction and tone of the passages of the hesitations, however, attempt to impress us with the immense importance of each new phase in the interchange, to the point where we become weary and defensive.

> . . . She looked at him, and oh, the weariness to her, of the effort to understand another language, the weariness of hearing him, attending to him, making out who he was, as he stood there fair-bearded and alien, looking at her. She knew something of him, of his eyes. But she could not grasp him. She closed her eyes. . . .
> . . . A new degree of anger came over him. What did it all matter? What did it matter if the mother talked Polish and cried in

labour, if this child were stiff with resistance and crying? Why take it to heart? Let the mother cry in labour, let the child cry in resistance, since they would do so. Why should he fight against it, why resist? Let it be, if it were so. Let them be as they were, if they insisted. (Pp. 70, 73)

We come to feel after page upon page of such passages of frantic contingent emotion that Lawrence has a formulary, or recipe, for expanding to apocalypse the minuitae of rather ordinary psychology. And when the lovers' relationship supposedly comes then to fruition, we are at a loss to discover what has happened to make things much different. All emotion, whether of love or hate or weariness has been so impassioned and intense before, the new experience seems just a degree of intensity greater. The switch to the even more frantic "nucleotic" prose tells us nothing in itself—it simply demands that we believe that the state desired has been achieved. But since the new, very different state is not rendered dramatically, only rhetorically, the gesturing of the characters supposedly in the condition is almost comic:

"You make me feel as if I was nothing," he said.

They were silent. She sat watching him. He could not move, his soul was seething and chaotic. She turned to her sewing again. But the sight of her bent before him held him and would not let him be. She was a strange, hostile, dominant thing. Yet not quite hostile. As he sat he felt his limbs were strong and hard, he sat in strength.

She was silent for a long time, stitching. He was aware, poignantly, of the round shape of her head, very intimate, compelling. She lifted her head and sighed. The blood burned in him, her voice ran to him like fire.

"Come here," she said, unsure.

For some moments he did not move. Then he rose slowly and went across the hearth. It required an almost deathly effort of volition, or of acquiescence. He stood before her and looked down at her. Her face was shining again, her eyes were shining again like terrible laughter. It was to him terrible, how she could be transfigured. He could not look at her, it burnt his heart.

"My love!" she said.

And she put her arms round him as he stood before her, round his thighs, pressing him against her breast. And her hands on him seemed to reveal to him the mould of his own nakedness, he was passionately lovely to himself. He could not bear to look at her. (Pp. 89–90)

The continuity of both style and substance in the middle sections of the book—dealing with Will and Anna—is as dubious as the rest. Early in the courtship Anna is excited by Will's love for church architecture: "He talked of Gothic and Renaissance and Perpendicular, and Early English and Norman. The words thrilled her." Later she resents intensely the competition for Will's spirit the cathedral offers—she wants him to have no meaningful life except through her. Yet in the final compromise that is their marriage, she gives up her own yearnings for "something beyond" (presented as a sad, limiting thing to do) while he sublimates his religious impulses in crafts and teaching. Having squelched herself and her husband, she is yet in some way "Anna Victrix" (though the epithet may be—and I wish it so—ironic, or even tragic, as in ". . . she knew she had won. And an ashy desolation came over her"). During their honeymoon they are at the "heart of eternity" and "unalterably glad." The truth of these absolute statements is questionable when we read of the wretched states they have yet to pass through and the melancholy they end in:

How passionately the Brangwens craved for it, the ecstasy. The father was troubled, dark-faced and disconsolate, on Christmas night, because the day was become as every day, and hearts were not aflame. Upon the mother was a kind of absentness, as ever, as if she were exiled for all her life. Where was the fiery heart of joy, now the coming was fulfilled; where was the star, the Magi's transport, the thrill of new being that shook the earth? (P. 278)

Tom Brangwen had come to his wife like an animal; they had fought and become tender. Will and his wife come to one another like birds of prey and it is apparently the thing desired:

> She wanted his eyes to come to hers, to know her. And they would not. They remained intent, and far, and proud, like a hawk's, naive and inhuman as a hawk's. So she loved him and caressed him and roused him like a hawk, till he was keen and instant, but without tenderness. He came to her fierce and hard, like a hawk striking and taking her. He was no mystic any more, she was his aim and object, his prey. And she was carried off, and he was satisfied, or satiated at last. (P. 159)

One wishes to say that this is the wrong kind of love, but this is the love that sustains them throughout:

> This was what their love had become, a sensuality violent and extreme as death. They had no conscious intimacy, no tenderness of love. It was all the lust and the infinite, maddening intoxication of the sense, a passion of death. (P. 234)

They are left in this dubious condition as we move on to the next generation, and as we leave we have no real idea what Lawrence wants us to think of the relationship. The experiences rendered have been heavily dualistic, the language absolutist. All that we do know for sure is that we have found it hard to swallow, almost comic, that Will, this provincial grammar school teacher, church sexton, squelched husband, is really "in the darkness potent with an overwhelming voluptuousness." We find hard to visualize an Anna who is at once all the following: (1) the daytime woman who "loves" children and wash (yet feeling unfulfilled, and resenting her daughter Ursula later on); (2) the naked ritualistic dancer; (3) the instinctual female animal who resents her husband's religious urges; (4) the oracular altruist who fights her husband only to help him ("She was relieved, she was free of him. She had given him to himself. She wept sometimes with tiredness and helplessness. But he was a husband," p. 187); and (5) the woman surprised and delighted to find her husband capable of wanting other women and of taking her merely physically and impersonally:

> In a kind of radiance, superb in her inscrutability, she laughed before him. She too could throw everything overboard, love, intimacy, responsibility. What were her four children to her now? What did it matter that this man was the father of her four children?
>
> He was the sensual male seeking his pleasure, she was the female ready to take hers: but in her own way. A man could turn into a free lance: so then could a woman. (P. 232)

Anna does not come through as a woman but as an essay, or better, as a compendium. Some pages back in the book Will was pictured as "potent with an overwhelming voluptuousness," but now as a "free lance" Anna likes him "better than the ordinary mute, half-effaced, half-subdued man she usually knew him to be. . . . she had been bored by the old husband." Obviously the two passages give different impressions as to what Anna previously thought of her husband. Again, irony may be allowed in one or other of the passages, but the reader cannot be sure where, because of the absolutist, passionate language of both.

Anna's daughter Ursula does not like her mother much, thinks her too much a breeder without "spirituality and stateliness." Either Lawrence or Ursula sees Anna as having "all the cunning of a breeding animal." Such language, if Lawrence's, hurts whatever respect we have left for Anna; if Ursula's, it gives Anna's daughter a frigidity that becomes typical of her throughout the novel. We read of her warmth, her social commitment, her spiritual aspirations, but again the language describing her "dark," selfish side is too absolutist to allow us to believe in these. The first of the following passages cannot live with the second:

> So her face grew more and more shut, and over her flayed, exposed soul of a young girl who had gone open and warm to give herself to the children, there set a hard, insentient thing, that worked mechanically according to a system imposed. . . .

But hard and fierce she had fastened upon him, cold as the moon and burning as a fierce salt. Till gradually his warm, soft iron yielded, yielded, and she was there fierce, corrosive, seething with his destruction, seething like some cruel, corrosive salt around the last substance of his being, destroying him, destroying him in the kiss. And her soul crystallised with triumph, and his soul was dissolved with agony and annihilation. So she held him there, the victim, consumed, annihiliated. She had triumphed: he was not any more. (Pp. 320, 395)

It is simply a defect in overstating one's case; if Ursula is not all diabolic corrosiveness and rampant will, the language of the second passage must be tempered from its absoluteness. Faced with the coldness of Ursula throughout, we find ourselves liking the deviates Winifred and Tom at least as much as her, which presumably cuts across Lawrence's wishes and his dialectic.

Long after Skrebensky has been "destroyed" (which happens early in the relationship), we find that they are still together and that despite his onetime destruction he and she are nonetheless capable of the heights of ecstasy:

He had not taken her yet. With subtle, instinctive economy, they went to the end of each kiss, each embrace, each pleasure in intimate contact, knowing subconsciously that the last was coming. It was to be their final entry into the source of creation. (P. 450)

Apparently it does not take very much (Skrebensky is enough) to get to the desired land:

Whither they had gone, she did not know. But it was as if she had received another nature. She belonged to the eternal, changeless place into which they had leapt together. (P. 451)

The question is irresistible: why is not constant reentry to the place possible if a Skrebensky, whom Ursula presumably dominates, is all that is necessary? For some reason it is necessary to have Ursula reject Skrebensky three different times in the novel. Can his repeatedly asserted weakness in reality be Ursula's? We are never sure; one can rarely tell prophecy from irony in Lawrence. Ursula's second tearful rejection of Skrebensky is followed by a letter in which, surprisingly, she prostrates herself before him: "I love the thought of you— once I am with you again, I shall ask no more than to rest in your shelter all my life" (P. 485). The absolutist language of triumphant dominance and exultant independence of previous scenes is rendered here either shabby or pathetic, whether one takes that language as Lawrence's or his character's.

And so then after Ursula recovers from an illness at the end of the book and it is said,

> But always, amid the ache of delirium, she had a dull firmness of being, a sense of permanency. She was in some way like the stone at the bottom of the river, inviolable and unalterable, no matter what storm raged in her body. Her soul lay still and permanent, full of pain, but itself forever. Under all her illness, persisted a deep inalterable knowledge. (P. 490)

We are less than convinced. We have become gun-shy and skeptical of absolutes. We do not trust "always," "permanency," "inviolable," "unalterable" any more. Nor can we trust Ursula's final rainbow vision. We will not predict that she will attain that condition though she is "sure" she will.

Back in chapter 10, there is a long sequence of meditation in the third person—it begins as Ursula's—on the Christian answer of abnegation of self as the answer to life. But gradually the prose soars to a first-person affirmation of self which is certainly Lawrence's:

> Can I not, then, walk this earth in gladness, being risen from sorrow? Can I not eat with my brother happily, and with joy kiss my beloved, after my resurrection, celebrate my marriage in the flesh with feastings, go about my business eagerly, in the joy of my fellows? Is heaven impatient for me, and bitter against this earth, that I should hurry off or that I should linger, pale and untouched. Is the flesh which was crucified become as poison to the crowds in the street, or is it as a strong gladness and hope to

them, as the first flower blossoming out of the earth's humus?
(P. 280)

The problems are Ursula's but the answers are Lawrence's,
here not in the rainbow symbology but in that of the biblical
style. Ursula asks the questions but she must experience much
before she has her rainbow vision (for what it's worth) at the
end of the book. Lawrence here sings out his answer impa-
tiently, character, voice, narrative sequence be damned.
When Lawrence declaims in his biblical style, as here, the
answer to the passage's opening question "Can I not, then,
walk this earth in gladness . . ?" is yes. But then much of the
rest of the book cries out no.

If now we go back to answer not Lawrence's, but those
critical questions posed at the beginning of this essay, I think
the novel has shown a dichotomy between what the styles
variously promise and what the book renders. The characters
do generalize and symbolize, if not the depth of human experience, certainly the fluctuations of the tremulous affective life.
Lawrence's "prophecy" is built up out of the knowledge of the
affective life and is a strange and confused melange of infinite
desires, frantic loves and hates, intense beliefs, radical skepti-
cisms, and an ever-lurking sense of tragic irony beneath the
prophetic certainty. Hence it is not coherent prophecy at all,
but a series of attitudes. Each has its own tone and style. Some
attitudes sing from the page, others rant. But they do not
choir.[2] Each pretends to absoluteness. And so the book is
radically discontinuous in tone. It strikes this reader much as
that beautifully evoked evening sky struck the young Tom
Brangwen:

> Then somewhere in the night a radiance again, like a vapour.
> And all the sky was teeming and tearing along, a vast disorder of
> flying shapes and darkness and ragged fumes of light and a great
> brown circling halo, then the terror of a moon running liquid-
> brilliant into the open for a moment, hurting the eyes before she
> plunged under cover of cloud again. (P. 44)

ᑋᔓ

Discontinuities of tone in a work of art are easier to explain than continuity to achieve, the flawed mind easier to analyze than the mind of genius. Genius in some ways Lawrence undoubtedly is. Were *The Rainbow* continuous in tone, rummaging about Lawrence's biography, his letters, his other works, would be an extraneous exercise. (It was, for instance, my experience in reviewing the "criticism" on Hart Crane's *The Bridge* that the continuity of the poem is not understood through a study of the terrible discontinuity of the poet's life. Were the poem a failure, the psychological implications of a life radically disjointed might be relevant in explanation. Most of the Crane literature, however, anticipates a flawed poem because of the flawed life, and is so not relevant.) In the remarks following, which use extrinsic data, I want to hypothesize that the stylistic discontinuities in *The Rainbow* that I have attempted to articulate above find their explanation in unstable metaphysical thought, an instability masked by absolutism and arrogance. The remarks are relevant only in so far as the analysis above is accurate.

Lawrence has been revered and damned for all sorts of metacritical reasons, for his social, sexual, political, and religious views. Such metacriticism has validity as metacriticism only, not as criticism, in so far as it is evaluating a given work not on the intrinsic *continuity* of the views within the work but on the simple *presence* of the views in the work (in so far, that is, as the reader sees Lawrence as a true or false prophet of a New Age of something or other). T. S. Eliot's strictures in *After Strange Gods* (with which I quite agree) are essentially metacritical, judging Lawrence for what does *not* appear in the works, for his humorlessness, and for the lack in his characters of much of a sense of moral obligation, humility, compassion, or pity. I prefer the metaphysics and the ethics of an Eliot to Lawrence's. But I must admit that I often find works of art of great continuity which lack the metacritical virtues I admire. Lawrence's *Rainbow*, however, is not one of them.

I believe Lawrencian metaphysics to be squarely within the posture of exultant dualism, as I have delineated the position in the previous chapter. And, as I tried to demonstrate there, I believe that the position has intrinsic contradictions inevitably leading to stylistic discontinuities which are subject to critical as well as to metacritical scrutiny.

The following passages from Lawrence's major metaphysical essay, "The Crown" (circa 1915, contemporaneous with *The Rainbow*, and reaffirmed in 1925—"It says what I still believe"), echo the Blakean tradition of exultant dualism, of marriages of Heaven and Hell, of Good and Evil:

> And there is no rest, no cessation from the conflict. For we are two opposites which exist by virtue of our inter-opposition. Remove the opposition and there is collapse, a sudden crumbling into universal nothingness. . . . It is the perfect opposition of dark and light that brindles the tiger with gold flame and dark flame. . . . And this supreme relation is made absolute in the clash and the foam of the meeting waves. And the clash and the foam are the Crown, the Absolute. . . .
>
> The crown is upon the perfect balance of the fight, it is not the fruit of either victory. The crown is not prize of either combatant. It is the *raison d'être* of both. It is the absolute within the fight. (*Phoenix* II, pp. 368, 373)

Darkness as perfect as the light, strife as perfect balance, the crown of life: such is the foundation of the exultant dualism posture—the pretense, in Sam Johnson's view, of going forward on the deepest problems of life while really only turning round (see above p. 64). The following embraces that other archetype of the exultant dualism position—the glorification of the "moment" of cosmic consciousness or being, as the only raison d'être of the life of the mortal ego:

> If I say that I *am*, this is false and evil. I am not. Among us all, how many have being?—too few. Our ready-made individuality, our identity is no more than an accidental cohesion in the flux of time. The cohesion will break down and utterly cease to be. The atoms will return into the flux of the universe. And that unit of cohesion which I was will vanish utterly.
>
> I am not immortal till I have achieved immortality. And immortality is not a question of time, of everlasting life. It is a question of consummate being. . . . When we have surged into

being, when we have caught fire with friction, we are the immortals of heaven . . . it is a question of conquering by divine grace, as the tiger leaps on the trembling deer, in utter satisfaction of the Self, in complete fulfilment of desire. . . . There is no ark, there is no eternal system, there is no rock of eternal truth. In Time and in Eternity all is flux. Only in the other dimension, which is not the time-space dimension, is there Heaven. We can no more *stay* in this heaven than the flower can stay on its stem. We come and go. (Pp. 384, 410–11, 413)

Combat, conflict, and friction as necessary to lead to the transient moment of heavenly consciousness: thus the sum of the Lawrencian metaphysic. Here too the intuitive underpinning of *The Rainbow*. Three generations of combative and frictional relationships which intermittently spark into moments of fulfillment for one or the other combatants; household morality as irrelevant to the individuals as to the tiger leaping on the deer—though to be sure, the more balanced the conflict, the more splendidly themselves the combatants, the surer the spark. The absolutist language of *The Rainbow* which the essay above finds discontinuous in context is now seen to apply to this transient "immortal" moment, though it makes allusions constantly through the biblical language to that other sort of immortality. Minimal solace pretending to maximal satisfaction of human desire through a deceptive rhetoric and an arrogant tone: the common failings of the exultant dualism position.

Stylistic discontinuity, then, as a manifestation of metacritical discontinuity of thought: the final result of the position. We are told time and again by Lawrence and his apologists that the nature of the "moment," since it is the product of the strife of opposites, can be rendered only by the language and imagery of contradiction, of polarity, antitheses, incompatibles, that the consciousness to be expressed through these means is in fact inexpressible, inexplicable, unarticulable. This state of affairs is a source of excitement to some critics, of bewilderment to others:

As transcriptions of the Underself, however, as an attempt to articulate the movements of something by its nature inarticulate and unarticulable, Lawrence's writing is on the whole elegant. Referred to the Underself and not to the self, passages that might otherwise repel grow suddenly luminous and right. . . . What Lawrence "means". . . should —if Lawrence is right and his method justified—remain unavailable to consciousness, unsayable in the categories of awareness in any direct way. This is frustrating. But by obvious definition, the unconscious content conveyed by the subjective correlatives is inexpressible except by way of other correlatives. And if the relative passages in Lawrence are valid, they ought to evoke, as I think they do, a correlative response in the reader, which should remain nevertheless somewhere beneath graspable consciousness in himself. (Alan Friedman, "The Other Lawrence," pp. 239ff.)

It is actually *from* the destructiveness (in this case disintegrative sensuality) that the creativeness, we are to believe, proceeds, or develops. . . . tensions as powerful as these are not to be resolved so neatly and rationally. For Lawrence is under an evident compulsion to make *incompatible* statements about voluptuousness or dissociated sensuality, and is struggling to find a novelistic pattern sufficiently flexible to allow him to do so. (Colin Clarke, *River of Dissolution*, pp. 53, 63)

Salvation issues as a call from the "unknown," and many seek but few are called. The most that any character can do is recognize the call when it issues from some inscrutable heart of life which can neither be named nor cognitively known.

The narrator knows all, sees all, but can deliver himself of the truth only in shadowy similitudes. The reader cannot challenge this outcome, because he is never in a position to develop an understanding of "folded centres of darkness" on his own. (Julian Moynahan, *The Deed of Life*, pp. 43, 48)

One can argue as Friedman does that the apparent stylistic discontinuities are really organic juxtapositionings of radically different modes of being. But the appeal is to our unconscious, or "Underself," of which he says we can know no thing consciously. This is a completely metacritical appeal, and completely unarguable and unprovable. *Critically* we can only say about Lawrence's brand of exultant dualism, as we have said about Blake's, Whitman's, and Thomas's, that nothing is done to reconcile the dualisms, the contraries of life (death, pain, strife, destruction) for those who find them evil and tragic, by calling them good, necessary, and right. And certainly nothing is done to convince that skeptical reader by being arrogant about such an answer, since it is admittedly an inexpressible reaction to an unknowable entity.

The posture of certitude in Lawrence seems to this reader in fact a mask for irresolution, confusion, and instability. I have tried to sketch how discontinuity in one's metaphysical thought can lead to discontinuities of style; the further step backward into explanations of the origins of an author's discontinuity of thought brings one to the very murky waters of psychological and biographical analysis. I do not feel that critics have had much to add to Eliot's assessment of Lawrence as a man bereft of a coherent social or personal context, who damns those contexts from which he is alienated while desiring the stability of such contexts, and so searches for substitute contexts (as those eccentric fabrications in the casting about of the later novels).

Eliot mentions too what he calls Lawrence's "distinct sexual morbidity." This is a theme which has had a great efflorescence. I quote but one diagnosis of Lawrence's "problem":

> I suggest that the discrepancy can best be explained in terms of a deep split in Lawrence himself. I believe that initially he made a strenuous effort to reconcile the male and female elements in himself but that he was unable to do so, that he was by nature more strongly feminine than masculine, and that his insistence in the *Fantasia* on an absolute degree of masculinity is evidence of an extreme reaction, a refusal even to acknowledge the existence of feminine components in his make-up. "The individual psyche divided against itself," wrote Lawrence, "divides the world against itself." . . . there are valid grounds for believing that Lawrence was divided against himself. . . . (H. M. Daleski, "The Duality of Lawrence," p. 11)

Lawrence's "effeminacy" and his ambivalent feelings toward his alleged homosexuality and toward various modes of sexual behavior have been popular approaches to the works since the

sixties, approaches used sometimes to damn the works, sometimes to praise them.[3] It was my experience that Hart Crane's
homosexuality neither hindered nor helped *The Bridge*—it simply did not enter in—though many critics psychologically
oriented based their (conflicting) analyses of the poem on the
biographical fact of homosexuality. Seeing *The Rainbow* as
flawed and discontinuous as I do, I can accept the idea that a
psychologically divided self in Lawrence either toward society
or toward sexuality has caused the discontinuities in thought
and style. But it is the analysis of the work that should pro-
voke such personal analysis of the artist, not, as so often happens, the other way around.

Notes

1. See Charles L. Ross's "The Revisions of the Second Generation in *The Rainbow*"
RES 107, (1976): 277–95 where the handling of Will and Anna is reluctantly labeled an
"artistic failure" and "incoherent" (p.288). It is made clear in Ross's essay that most of
the language of absolutes is added in later drafts.

2. *Cf.* the positions of Graham Hough, *The Dark Sun* (N. Y. 1957); Roger Sale,
"The Narrative Technique of *The Rainbow*," *Modern Fiction Studies* 5 (Spring 1959); S.
L. Goldberg, "*The Rainbow*: Fiddlebow and Sand," *Essays in Criticism* 11 (October
1961.)

3. See Mark Spilka, "Lawrence Up-Tight," *Novel* 4 (Spring 1971); David Cavitch,
D. H. Lawrence and the New World (N. Y. 1969), esp. pp. 29–30; J. Meyers, "Lawrence
and Homosexuality," in *D. H. Lawrence : Novelist, Poet, Prophet*, ed. Stephen Spender
(New York, 1973).

5
Cultural Discontinuity in the Works of Kahlil Gibran

The Prophet has been among us since 1923; by 1976 the volume of counsels had been bought in America alone by more than six million people, read certainly by triple that many. The book has been too highly praised by the True Believers, but it also has been too roundly and imprecisely attacked. Gibran was a man of considerable talents, and a critical sketch of his work and life is in order after a half century both to correct these imprecisions and to probe the actual merits and defects in the works.[1] Many of those merits and defects are intimately bound to Gibran's struggle to live within two cultures, the Lebanese and the American. In Gibran's case, the struggle led him to adopt the pseudo-wisdom posture of exultant dualism with which the two previous chapters have dealt. Gibran's personal psychic suffering in maintaining the posture before his different audiences is variously demonstrated in some of his best, certainly most poignant, lyrical moments. These lyric passages, which constitute the most authentic Gibran, dramatize the pangs of cultural discontinuity. Gibran's life and work and the small body of critical comment on that life and work are so little and poorly known, despite the popularity of *The Prophet*, that I find it necessary for the purposes of this chapter to outline both.

There has appeared a reliable biography of Gibran by Jean and Kahlil (the writer's cousin and namesake) Gibran (New York Graphic Society, 1974) that goes a long way toward the necessary demystification of Gibran. The work had already in part been accomplished—brilliantly I think—in 1934 by Mikhail Naimy, a writer of great stature in the Middle East, in an impressionistic critical biography is Arabic. The book appeared in English, translated by the author, in 1950 (Philosophical Library), too late and little known, it seems, to counter the still fashionable tendencies to either deify or damn Gibran. One will learn from either biography that Kahlil Gibran is best, most realistically, understood as a Lebanese-American émigré writer, not as an oriental wise man.[2]

Born of Christian parents in the Lebanon in 1883, Gibran in 1895 was brought over to Boston's immigrant South End together with his brother and two sisters by their revered mother. They came partly to escape the poverty and restrictions of Ottoman rule, partly to escape from a drunken husband and father. Gibran, then a poor and uneducated boy of thirteen, wandered into the Denison Settlement House on Tyler Street. A social worker there, Jessie Fremont Beale, when apprised of Kahlil's talent for drawing, wrote to a friend of hers, Fred Holland Day, asking if he would assist the boy. It was Day, an eminent publisher (Copeland and Day), photographer, collector, and man of taste, who developed the boy's talents for draftsmanship and his attitudes toward the arts. It was Day who had Gibran read Blake, Keats, Shelley, Emerson, and Whitman, and various turn-of-the-century British, American, and Continental poets. Day was fascinated by Gibran's Near-Eastern heritage, which was Christian, not Islamic, and thus partly kin to the Western Tradition. Day apparently encouraged the impressionable young man to be proud of that heritage. Gibran as a consequence went with some enthusiasm back to Lebanon for three years of advanced secondary schooling in a Maronite-Christian school in Beirut. Before he left for Lebanon at the age of fifteen, Gibran had already sold some book-cover designs to Scribners, and, by his own account, had been inveigled into a love affair with a patroness of the arts. He left for Lebanon having just met and been struck by the young poet, Josephine Preston Peabody, who was about to be published by Copeland and Day. Gibran came back to Boston in 1902 and at the age of nineteen had to face the deaths in quick succession of a sister, brother, and mother. Terribly bereaved and weighed down with a melancholy which later became the ground bass of all his work, the young Gibran found companionship, both spiritual and cultural, with Miss Peabody.

The immigrant boy of nineteen knew what he wanted: to be a "pure artist" in the sense of the term as understood by Day and Peabody. But he had no money, was living with, and was supported by, his sister and her needle, and had a command of English rather more comic than sufficient. An exhibition of his drawings was arranged by Fred Day in Day's own studio in 1904, and to that exhibition came a friend of Miss Peabody's, a Mary Haskell, headmistress of Miss Haskell's School for Girls, later the Cambridge School. Immediately taken by the drawings, Mary Haskell made the acquaintance of Gibran, and by 1908 was so convinced of his "genius" that she was willing to finance a year's schooling in art for him in Paris.

Gibran had by 1908, at the age of twenty-five, published two books of short fiction in Arabic and dozens of short poetic essays in Arab-American newspapers. He was well known in literary circles in both the Near East and in the New York-Boston Lebanese-American community as one of the vanguard of artists who were infusing Western attitudes and modes into Arabic literature but felt himself stalemated as a painter from lack of formal training. With the Haskell offer for Paris began the spiritual and patronage relationship between Mary Haskell and Gibran that was to last into the twenties, and indeed beyond Gibran's death in 1931. Mary Haskell kept voluminous journals during all of these years (now deposited at the library of the University of North Carolina); these journals are a mine of information about Gibran, and are the primary source for the biography by Jean and Kahlil Gibran. From these journals emerge two very decent people: Mary, deeply committed to things of the spirit—art, ethics, humanitarianism—and afraid of sexuality; Gibran, deeply grateful, eager to please, puzzled and uncertain of his role with Mary. Was he to worship, or teach, or love, or marry this admirable woman? What did she want; what was the decent thing to do? One learns much about Gibran through Mary's eyes; yet one must also be cautious about Mary's Gibran. It seems clear from Gibran's writings, his letters, and in other accounts of the man, that there is much in Gibran, the Lebanese Gibran, that did not find expression in the relationship with Mary Haskell. Gibran proposed to Mary, and was rejected. Whether for this reason or for wider artistic horizons or both, Gibran, in 1912, left Boston for a studio apartment on West Tenth Street in New York City and remained there for the rest of his life.

The early New York years were overcast for Gibran by the terrible fate of Lebanon during the Great War. (Fully one-third of the population of the Mountain starved). His chronic melancholia pervades the prose poems in Arabic of this period. But he was finding success in America, where he wanted it most, with both his symbolical drawings and his drawings from life of famous artists and other notables. He began now his experiments in writing in English, aided mightily by Mary Haskell. His early parables, which stemmed far more from Old and New Testament sources than from anything in Islamic literature, gained much critical attention, especially through the pages of the prestigious *Seven Arts Magazine*. The publication in 1918 of the collection of parables in English, *The Madman*, and the delayed publication of *The Procession* in Arabic in 1919 mark a watershed for Gibran. Though his reputation in the Arabic world grew in the twenties as a result of further collections of his earlier prose poems in Arabic, Gibran now turned all of his literary energies to the slim books (all with Alfred A. Knopf) of poems, parables, and aphorisms in English, and his draftsmanship to the illustration of these books.

The continuity of tone that runs throughout the works of Gibran is that of lonely alienation yearning for connections. Beneath all his prophetic masks, Gibran's lyric cry for connection is his most authentic voice. Hungering for real unity, Gibran is ever attempting to lift himself up by his own bootstraps, to deliver truths or at least prolegomena to the multitudes in old societies or new, or to come, on social and cosmic questions. But ever behind these pronunciamentos is the Gibran of unsureness, of profound melancholy, of tragic vision. Gibran is at home neither in the old cultures nor the new, and an unresolved dualism vitiates much of the work when, as so often occurs, it pretends to resolution. This is a pattern typical of what I have termed in the previous chapters the posture of exultant dualism within the Western romantic condition.

The reader of the translations from the Arabic and of the English works of Gibran will find in each a confusing series of self-projections and investitures. Gibran would be, in the mold of William Blake, both angry social reformer of old cultural contexts and prophet of an expanding cosmic consciousness beyond any need of a given cultural context. But he emerges most often and fundamentally as lonely poet finding solace only in the poetic consciousness or imagination. He wants desperately to trumpet a humanism with absolutist foundations, but at the center of his vision (a center he keeps trying to shroud in mist) he is a tragic dualist:

> We are the sons of Sorrow; we are the poets
> And the prophets and the musicians. We weave
> Raiment for the goddess from the threads of
> Our hearts.
>
> ("We And You," *Secrets of the Heart*, p. 41)

> And Wisdom opened her lips and spoke:
> "You, Man, would see the world with the eyes of God, and would grasp the secrets of the hereafter by means of human thought. Such is the fruit of ignorance. . . .
> "The many books and strange figures and the lovely thoughts around you are ghosts of the spirits that have been before you. The words your lips utter are the links in the chain that binds you and your fellow man.
>
> ("A Visit from Wisdom," *A Second Treasury*, p. 37)

My departure was like Adam's exodus from Paradise, but the Eve of my heart was not with me to make the whole world an Eden.

That night, in which I had been born again, I felt that I saw
death's face for the first time.
Thus the sun enlivens and kills the fields with its heat.

(*Broken Wings*, p. 47)

Though the child was dead, the sounds of the
drinking cups increased in the hall. . . .
He was born at dawn and died at sunrise. . . .
A lily that has just blossomed from the bud of
life and is mashed under the feet of death.
A dear guest whose appearance illuminated
Selma's heart and whose departure killed her soul.
This is the life of men, the life of nations, the
life of suns, moons and stars.

(*Broken Wings*, pp. 118–19)

The passages are I think "touchstones" for the central drama
of Gibran's soul, a dualism that longs for unity, a belief only
in the "divinity" of man's ability to create and to love, and a
struggle to "make do" with this humanism. It is the humanism
of Gibran's mentor, William Blake, the humanism of Percy
Shelley before his disillusionment (see above pp. 52–57). The
young poet aspires to the energy of Blake, the social ardency
of the early Shelley, the cosmic euphoria of the Whitman of
the *Song of Myself*; what Gibran really achieves, however, are
dramatizations of the inextricable dualisms he found in the
Songs of Innocence and Experience, the tragic tone of Shelley's *The
Triumph of Life*, the solitary laments of "Out of the Cradle," or
"When Lilacs Last." Gibran knew a good deal of the major
romantic literature of the West, knew well and often uses
motifs from the poets mentioned and others, especially Keats,
in that tradition.

Gibran struggled always to extricate himself from a melan-
cholic position, at times by a shell of toughness and bitterness
that seemed fashioned after Nietzsche, at times by a brand of
transcendentalism that seems a fusion of his own intuitions
with his knowledge of Emerson, Naimy, and others. Neither
role convinces as much as does the lyric voice of the poet who
is often ashamed of both roles.

The bitter Yusif El Fakhri, in the philosophic dialogue "The Tempest," has withdrawn from civilization, and he tells the questioning poet:

> "No, my brother, I did not seek solitude for religious purposes, but solely to avoid the people and their laws, their teachings and their traditions, their ideas and their clamour and their wailing. . . . What I really know to be true is the crying of my inner self. I am here living, and in the depths of my existence there is a thirst and hunger, and I find joy in partaking of the bread and wine of Life from the vases which I make and fashion by my own hands.

> (*Secrets of the Heart*, pp. 15, 20)

But though Fakhri sought solitude only to avoid civilization, he has had "religious" experiences:

> "And among all vanities of life, there is only one thing that the spirit loves and craves. One thing dazzling and alone. . . . It is an awakening in the spirit; it is an awakening in the inner depths of the heart; it is an overwhelming and magnificent power that descends suddenly upon man's conscience and opens his eyes, whereupon he sees Life amid a dizzying shower of brilliant music, surrounded by a circle of great light, with man standing as a pillar of beauty between the earth and the firmament. . . ."

> (P. 22)

Such momentary psychic experience is not to be denied; Gibran's poetry is often of such moments. The question is whether in Gibran's mind such moments of "mysticism" or "cosmic consciousness" are in fact intuitive glimpses into a higher reality for an immortal soul or but aesthetic apprehensions of the evolutionary potential in man's creative imagination. And the truth of the matter, demonstrably so, is that Gibran was tortured by the question, wanting to assert the one, while believing the other.

The poet's dilemma is indicated in any number of pieces in both the Arabic and English writings. *The Procession* consists of an internal debate between Age's desire to make sense of things and Youth's disdain for all formulation:

The truth of the flute will e'er remain,
While crimes and men are but disdain. . . .

Singing is love and hope and desire,
The moaning flute is the light and fire. . . .

Give me the flute and let me sing;
Forget what we said about everything.
Talk is but dust, speckling the
Ether and losing itself in the vast
Firmament. . . .

Why do you not renounce the
Future and forget the past?
(*Secrets of the Heart*, pp. 150, 155, 157, 158)

Fakhri's bitterness and "Youth's" bitterness, and also their aestheticism or mysticism, are reflected again in another internal debate, *The Earth Gods*, a poem in English finished and published just before Gibran's death but sketched out in the same period, 1912–18, which seems to be the time of greatest ferment, turmoil, and creativity for Gibran. Indeed most of *The Prophet* was written in 1918, though not published till 1923. The reason Gibran often gave for delay of *The Prophet* was that he wanted to make the book as perfect as he could. A profound unsureness about whether he was in fact prophet or "false alarm" (as he once confessed he felt to Mikhail Naimy), prophetic "forerunner" or mere bitter "wanderer," is more likely the reason.

There is a very moving and revealing Arabic poem of nightmare, confession, and self-analysis called "Between Night and Morning" in the *Tempests* volume of 1920. The poem consists of two related nightmares. The first is of the poet's harvesting fruit trees of his own planting. After the harvest is given away to the people (his Arabic reader, specifically the Christian-Lebanese), the poet discovers his fruit is as bitter as gall:

Woe to me, for I have placed a
Curse in the mouths of the people, and an
Ailment in their bodies.
(*Secrets of the Heart*, p. 60)

Another tree is planted "in a field afar from the path of Time," watered with "blood and tears," but not one of the people will now taste of this sweet fruit of sadness, and the poet withdraws to his solitude. The second nightmare is of a boat of the poet's own building, "empty . . . except of rainbow colors":

> and I said to
> Myself, "I shall return with the empty
> Boat of my thoughts to the harbour of the
> Isle of my birth."
> . . .And on the masts and
> On the rudder I drew strange figures that
> Compelled the attention and dazzled the
> Eye. And as I ended my task, the boat of
> My thoughts seemed as a prophetic vision
> Sailing between the two infinites, the
> Sea and the sky.

(Pp. 61–62)

And the people *are* dazzled:

> Such welcome was mine because my boat
> Was beautifully decorated, and none
> Entered and saw the interior of the
> Boat of my thoughts, nor asked what
> I had brought from beyond the seas. Nor
> Could they observe that I had brought
> My boat back empty. . . .

(P. 62)

The guilty poet then sails the seas to fill his boat with worthy cargo, but his people will not welcome him back, though the boat is full. And he withdraws, unable to speak or sing, even as dawn approaches. Both nightmares are obvious allegories of Gibran's guilt feelings with regards to his art and his audience. Gibran later, at the full tide of success of *The Prophet*, was confiding to Mary Haskell his plans for sequels, in which Almustafa, back at the isle of his birth, is first rejected by his disciples and then stoned to death by "his people" in a market place.

The "Seven Selves" parable is likewise deeply personal and poignant, as are others in *The Madman*, *The Forerunner*, and *The Wanderer*:

> "Ah! could I but be like one of you, a self with a determined lot! But I have none, I am the do-nothing self, the one who sits in the dumb, empty nowhere and nowhen, while you are busy re-creating life". . . . the seventh self remained watching and gazing at nothingness, which is behind all things.
>
> ("The Seven Selves," *The Madman*, p. 23)

The "Forerunner" preaches new gospel of a new John the Baptist to his people, but as he closes he exclaims:

> "Like moths that seek destruction in the flame you gather daily in my garden: and with faces uplifted and eyes enchanted you watch me tear the fabric of your days. And in whispers you say the one to the other, 'He sees with the light of God. He speaks like the prophets of old. . . .'
>
> "Aye, in truth, I know your ways, but only as an eagle knows the ways of his fledglings. And I fain would disclose my secret. Yet in my need for your nearness I feign remoteness, and in fear of the ebbtide of your love I guard the floodgates of my love."
>
> After saying these things the Forerunner covered his face with his hands and wept bitterly.
>
> (*The Forerunner*, pp. 63–64)

And then later after the coming of the "prophet," and also the commentary on both the historical Jesus and the Jesus within (*Jesus, Son of Man*, 1926), Gibran projects himself as the "Wanderer":

> I met him at the crossroads, a man with but a cloak and a staff, and a veil of pain upon his face. . . . what I now record was born out of the bitterness of his days though he himself was kindly, and these tales are of the dust and patience of his road.
>
> (*The Wanderer*, p. 3)

It is within this melancholy context that the record of Gibran's euphoric moments and the quasi-theology he fashions around those moments must be read.

The Prophet is an extended flight on the wings of the dubious idea which Gibran derived from Blake, Whitman, and Nietzsche, that the evolving godliness in man is god enough for exultant worship:

> My God, my aim and my fulfilment; I am
> thy yesterday and thou art my tomorrow.
> I am thy root in the earth and thou art
> my flower in the sky.
>
> (*The Madman*, p. 10)

> You are your own forerunner, and the towers
> you have builded are but the foundation of
> your giant-self. And that self too shall be
> a foundation. . . .
> O my faith, my untamed knowledge, how shall I
> fly to your height and see with you man's
> larger self pencilled upon the sky?
>
> (*The Forerunner*, pp. 7, 39)

The "Greater Self," "Larger Self," "Vast Man" (cf. Blake's "Eternal Great Humanity Divine," above, p. 53) within us is the God of *The Prophet* (and, to be sure, of *Jesus, Son of Man*):

> But your god-self dwells not alone in your being.
> Much in you is still man, and much in you is not yet man. . . .
> Like a procession you walk together towards your god-self.
> You are the way and the wayfarers. . . .
> In your longing for your giant self lies your goodness: and that
> longing is in all of you. . . .
> For what is prayer but the expansion of yourself into the living
> ether? . . .
> Our God, who art our winged self, it is thy will in us that willeth.
>
> (*The Prophet*, pp. 39, 40, 66, 67, 68)

All of which may seem acceptable doctrine in some theological (Emersonian) circles, however in other (particularly Lebanese-

Christian) circles, it is heretical because the position wants (1) to do without a Godhead existing independently of man while pretending to the absolute authority of such, and (2) to do without any promise of ego-immortality while pretending sufficient compensation in the immortality of the life force, that is, in the succeeding generations of "Man" evolving an ever wider and wider consciousness.

Whitman's "Myself" is much the same as Gibran's "Larger Self." In fact, *The Prophet* is deeply influenced by the *Song of Myself*.[3] Both are devious enough to obscure the problem of evil in the euphoric, cosmic moment:

> What is called good is perfect, and what is called sin is just as
>   perfect.
>
> > (Whitman, "To Think of Time")

> For what is evil but good tortured by its own hunger and thirst?
> > (*The Prophet*, p. 64)

Both are honest enough to dramatize the endless pain in the contingent reality:

> The malformed limbs are tied to the anatomist's table,
> What is removed drops horribly into a pail. . . .
> > (*Song of Myself*, sec. 15)

> For even as love crowns you so shall he crucify you. . . .
> Your blood and my blood is naught but the sap that feeds the
>   tree of heaven.
> > (*The Prophet*, pp. 11, 23)

In both the *Song of Myself* and *The Prophet* we have in fact dualism pretending to unity. The following is perhaps Gibran's best expression of his true position:

> Verily all things move within your being in constant half embrace, the desired and the dreaded, the repugnant and the cherished, the pursued and that which you would escape.

These things move within you as lights and shadows in pairs that cling.

And when the shadow fades and is no more, the light that lingers becomes a shadow to another light.

And thus your freedom when it loses its fetters becomes itself the fetter of a greater freedom.

(*The Prophet*, p. 49)

This is a vision of a dualistic spiral; the wider the consciousness is expanded, the greater the awareness of *both* joy and pain, good and evil. Gibran's Arabic prose poem "The Ambitious Violet" is of a violet that would be a rose for a day so as to have a moment in the sun, a rose that is willing then to be dashed by the tempest. Or, as Gibran's "Jesus" says it, "The lilies and the brier live but a day, yet that day is eternity spent in freedom" (p. 54). One need not deemphasize the importance of ecstatic psychic or mystic moments to protest that a moment in eternity is a different blessing than to be eternally in eternity. Thus the bluff one often senses in both Gibran and Whitman. What is moving in both poets is their otherwhere tortured consciousness of this bravado. It is not, however, a bravado likely to bluff the Christian-Lebanese peasant in general, or the Christian-Lebanese peasant in Gibran.

In what is in many ways a more satisfying work than *The Prophet*, Gibran's late *The Earth Gods*, the "second god" strikes the true tonality of the artist-as-only-savior central to Gibran:

In our eyes is the vision that turns man's soul to flame,
And leads him to exalted loneliness and rebellious prophecy,
And on to crucifixion.
Man is born to bondage,
And in bondage is his honor and his reward. . . .
For deaf is the ear of the infinite,
And heedless is the sky.
We are the beyond and we are the Most High,
And between us and boundless eternity
Is naught save our unshaped passion
And the motive thereof.

(*The Earth Gods*, pp. 16, 25)

The first god speaks only of weariness and bitterness and death-wish; the third god speaks of merely human dancers and mere human love, ever fresh. All three gods represent attitudes of the poet in a complex inner debate with no possible resolution save that all three are capable of being taken momentarily by the beauty of the young lovers and by their dance in the ancient "sacred grove":

> Yea, what of this love of man and woman?
> See how the east wind dances with her dancing feet,
> And the west wind rises singing with his song.
> Behold our sacred purpose now enthroned,
> In the yielding of a spirit that sings to a body that dances.
> *(The Earth Gods,* "second god," p. 32)

The third god would build some transcendental truths upon this love, but the second god protests:

> Your hands have spun man's soul
> From living air and fire,
> Yet now you would break the thread,
> And lend your versèd fingers to an idle eternity. . . .
> Oh, lofty dreaming brother,
> Return to us from time's dim borderland!
> Unlace your feet from no-where and no-when,
> And dwell with us in this security.
>
> (Pp. 21, 35)

For the gods are "earth-bound." The poem ends with the third god finally agreeing with his brother:

> Better it is for us, and wiser,
> To seek a shadowed nook and sleep in our earth divinity,
> And let love, human and frail, command the coming day.
> (P. 41)

The voice of the lyric Gibran here persuades the prophetic Gibran; the poet persuades the transcendental philosopher.

The passage from *The Earth Gods* beginning "Oh, lofty dreaming brother" is a conscious variation on a motif in *The Prophet:*

And others among you called unto me, not in words, and they
said,
"Stranger, stranger, lover of unreachable heights, why dwell
you among the summits where eagles build their nests?
Why seek you the unattainable?
What storms would you trap in your net,
And what vaporous birds do you hunt in the sky?
Come and be one of us.
Descend and appease your hunger with our bread and quench
your thirst with our wine."

(P. 90)

Gibran's answer to the people in the grandiose manner of *The
Prophet* is that "I hunted only your larger selves" (p. 91). It is
in *The Wanderer* later that the motif receives its most personal
variation:

Two men were walking in the valley, and one man pointed with
his finger toward the mountain side, and said, "See you that
hermitage? There lives a man who has long divorced the world.
He seeks but after God, and naught else upon this earth."
And the other man said, "He shall not find God until he leaves his
hermitage, and the aloneness of his hermitage, and returns to our
world, to share our joy and pain, to dance with our dancers at the
wedding feast, and to weep with those who weep around the
coffins of our dead."
And the other was convinced in his heart, though in spite of his
conviction he answered, "I agree with all that you say, yet I
believe the hermit is a good man. And may it not well be that one
good man by his absence does better than the seeming goodness of
these many men?"

(P. 87)

More human? Yes. But Gibran is always partly thus. Gibran
the Christian-Lebanese peasant son worships the idea of the
Mother in *Broken Wings* (Bantam ed., pp. 82–83); Gibran the
philosopher of the larger self tells parents to stay out of their
children's way in *The Prophet* (pp. 17–18).

Gibran was born into an ancient and rich hill-culture in the
Lebanese Mountain (see below pp. 134–35) and he was both

separated from and separated himself from it. Thus the ambiguous love-hate, accusatory-guilty relationship of Gibran
with the old country and its (his) people:

> And he looked upon his mariners and said: "And what have I
> brought them? A hunter was I, in a distant land. With aim and
> might I have spent the golden arrows they gave me, but I have
> brought down no game. . . .
> And he ceased from speaking and there fell a deep gloom upon the
> nine, and their heart was turned away from him, for they under-
> stood not his words.
> And behold, the three men who were mariners longed for the sea;
> and they who had served in the Temple yearned for the consola-
> tion of her sanctuary; and they who had been his playfellows
> desired the market-place. They all were deaf to his words. . . .
> And behold, they turned and went every man to his own place, so
> that Almustafa, the chosen and the beloved, was left alone.
>
> (*The Garden of The Prophet*, pp. 5, 49–50)

The passages, as usual, allow for the accusing of the people
while in large measure dramatizing the self-accusation of the
poet. In one of the saddest parables in *The Wanderer*, ironically
and consciously given the title "Tears and Laughter," which is
the title of his first volume of Arabic prose poems, a crocodile
and a hyena protest that the people do not care when the
crocodile really cries or the hyena really laughs.

The fundamental tone of Gibran then is lyric, tragic,
alienated, punctuated by a series of struggles for tran-
scendence and/or involvement. (It is worth noting that Gibran's art work, too, his drawings, oils, washes, whatever merit
they have standing alone before the artist's eye, are deeply
illustrative of his fundamental tonality, pain and alienation
and longing pervading them almost to the exclusion of any
sense of joy.) Gibran is hardly a Blake or Whitman, not having
their linguistic and imagistic vitality (though his style—
obviously dependent on the King James Bible—is of considerable emotive and evocative power). But their "transcendental" thinking is much alike, often embracing the
exultant dualism which is a pretense of an achieved unity

covering a morass of conflicts. All three poets labor under the burden of their transcendent self-projections of unitary truth, and are wholly convincing only when wholly absorbed in dramatizations of their dualistic experiences. To put Gibran in this company, at least in terms of similarity of theme and substance, is both to save him from his cultists and to place him, rightly, far more within the Western than the Eastern poetic tradition.

With regard to Gibran's stature with "his people," the Arabic world in general perhaps, but more specifically the Christian-Lebanese and Lebanese-American worlds, there is a great deal of pride in the native son, and an appreciation of his bringing forms and themes of Western Romanticism into Arabic Literature. There are also negative reactions. Some predictable arch-conservatism, against which Gibran wrote and thrived. But also a thoughtful conservatism (for example, the letters to Gibran of the writer May Ziadeh) which sensed that beneath the bravado of the prophetic robes, Gibran had really no adequate replacement for the richness of the cultural heritage, both peasant and intellectual, of the Christian East, that the bread and wine in the hill village in Lebanon is perhaps a better bet for a life than the winds of solitude at the top of a mystic mountain, or the studio apartment at West Tenth Street in Manhattan. Gibran himself wrote with pain of this "exile":

> No punishment more severe has befallen a child of God; no exile so bitter. . . .

> We may be wealthier than the villagers in gold, but they are infinitely richer in fullness of true existence. . . .

> Oh, Giver of Graces, hidden from me behind these edifices of the throngs which are naught but idols and images. . . . hear the anguished cries of my imprisoned soul! Hear the agonies of my bursting heart! Have mercy and return Your straying child to the mountainside, which is Thy edifice! ("Contemplations in Sadness," *Secrets of the Heart*, pp. 144–45)

The involutions of Gibran, the fact that he put on so many masks, including this one—if this one is a mask—constitutes a human drama that is deeply moving, despite its having been often played: the drama of a talented émigré at home neither in the old country nor in the new.

Notes

1. Works originally in Arabic are: *Nymphs of the Valley* (1906); *Spirits Rebellious* (1908); *Broken Wings* (1912); *Tears and Laughter* (1914); *The Procession* (1919); *The Tempests* (1920); *Best Things* (1923); *Spiritual Sayings* (1927); *The Spikes of Grain* (1929).

Works originally in English are: *The Madman* (1918); *The Forerunner* (1920); *The Prophet* (1923); *Sand and Foam* (1926); *Jesus, the Son of Man* (1928); *The Earth Gods* (1931); *The Wanderer* (1932); *The Garden of Prophet* (1933), a posthumous compilation, all with A. A. Knopf. Most of the Arabic writings of Gibran have been collected in *A Treasury* and *A Second Treasury of Kahlil Gibran* (New York: Citadel Press, 1951, 1962), translated by Anthony R. Ferris. The translations make readable English prose, and I think a comparison of these with those of others will bring the reader back to Ferris's work. A good selection from the pieces in the two volumes is the Signet paperback, *Secrets of the Heart*, which together with the Bantam paperback of the novella, *Broken Wings*, is perhaps a sufficient sampling of Gibran's Arabic writings for the English reader. What these volumes lack for the critical reader is a chronological arrangement or even a dating of the various pieces.

2. The biography by Jean and Kahlil Gibran, cited above, is very helpful for Gibran's Boston years, less so for the New York City years. The book in general has a sense of incompleteness with respect to the Arabic side of Gibran's life. It is most comfortable when working with documents like letters and diaries: "Previous allusions to relationships and incidents that have not been corroborated by primary source material have remained unmentioned" (p.4). This procedure might be well in the biography of a man long dead, but the chaste avoidance of the very much alive Lebanese and Syrians and others in Boston and New York City that knew Gibran or knew of him thins the biography.

Mikhail Naimy's critical biography, cited above, for all of its impressionism and imprecisions gives the reader a more three-dimensional Gibran, one that seems more like the author of the works. There is a great deal more energy in the analyses of the works and actually a great deal more empathy for them than in the later biography. There is to be sure a great deal of Naimy in Naimy's book; he is using Gibran as an example of the backsliding initiate into the mysteries in which he is full professor, but the work at the same time has excitement, ironic self-awareness, and, I think, fundamental truthfulness to Gibran that gives it stature both as literary criticism and as creative achievement.

Khalil Hawi's *Kahlil Gibran: His Background, Character, and Works* (Beirut: American University of Beirut, 1963) is a very sober and intelligent study, and one that is critical both of Naimy's biography and Gibran's thought. But he is also respectful of Naimy's critical ability and of Gibran's contributions to Arabic literature. A well-known poet and scholar in the Arab world, Hawi was without benefit of the Haskell papers which would have gone some way toward clearing his objections to Naimy. Many of Hawi's objections to Naimy's book are rebutted in Nadeem Naimy's *Mikhail Naimy: An Introduction* (Beirut: American University of Beirut, 1967) and in Naimy's own *Sab'un* (transl. *Seventy*, Beirut: 1960).

The argument over Naimy's biography is not trivial (indeed it is still current in the Arab world) because the flaws Naimy—a man who seems to love and understand Gibran—finds in Gibran's character, weaknesses for women, money, fame, alcohol, in fact make Gibran more warmly human and the works more poignant. It seems clear from Gibran's letters (see *The Second Treasury*) that Naimy was indeed Gibran's closest comrade, and so I see no reason to assume that the "imaginary conversations" in Naimy's biography are not reconstructions of confidences given by Gibran over the years to Naimy.

Barbara Young did Gibran no favor with her fulsome *This Man From Lebanon* (New York: Knopf, 1945), as such cult material provokes understandably extreme reactions like that of Stefan Kanfer in the *New York Times Magazine* (25 June 1972). Kanfer, sensitive to many of the inadequacies of *The Prophet*, takes then the liberties of wide inaccuracies about Gibran's life, gratuitous witticisms, and simple obliviousness to the lyric Gibran behind the prophetic mask.

3. Suhail Hanna's "Gibran and Whitman: Their Literary Dialogue" (*Literature East and West*, 7:174–98) is a fine essay on the Whitman and New England Transcendentalism influence on Gibran.

6
Ethical Discontinuity in Henry James's *The Golden Bowl*

My homage to William James is in chapter 1 and elsewhere in this book; let me hasten to pay similar homage to Henry James before my remarks about limitations I find in *The Golden Bowl*. The two brothers together greatly increased the range and depth of American culture and civilization at the turn of the last century. Henry James took as his province the dramatization of special problems of the modern consciousness which we have come to know in large measure through him and others who have come after him in this century. I have tried in previous chapters of this book to outline two sorts of response to these special problems in the literature of this and the last century. Henry James, it is becoming clearer as the decades go by, was profoundly involved, as was his brother, in the implications of one of those responses, the idea of illusion as value. Inevitable in such a response are the ambivalences and ambiguities of Henry James; unnecessary, however, for such a response are the evasions and mystifications that sometimes occur in James and do not work to render the complexity of the situation, but to muddle it.

The critical entourage trailing *The Golden Bowl* is of that same diversity and apposition one finds behind *The Turn of the Screw* and indeed behind most of James's late work. All the permutations in ranking the four major characters as to moral worth have been exhausted in the critical evaluations. The work strikes one as a mystifying hall of mirrors where what one "knows" is continually distorted by what one further "sees." Or, to play with James's figure, any particular view of the situation presented in the novel is as one position of a screw in a board: twist the screw and all the relationships alter to a new position which causes our view of the situation to alter accordingly. There are innumerable possible positions and so innumerable points of view. The mirror or the screw as an analogy for the permanent bewilderment in groping for knowledge of good and evil is probably apt in suggesting the true obsessions and intentions of the late James. These intentions, these attitudes toward experience create the complex tone of *The Golden Bowl*. Dramatizing these attitudes is the continuous intention of the late James.

Yet I have reservations about the ultimate continuity of the tone of the novel. In the intent to dramatize the bewildering aspects of experience, James falters by making his characters at times rather repugnant, or shocking, or discontinuous to the reader.[1]

The Golden Bowl is not really "about" an adultery, per se, rather it is about paradoxical psychological conditions that obtain in all important situations of life: belief and doubt, simplicity and duplicity, "freedom" and "safety," seeing and knowing, what it is to have "everything" and "nothing." We are given a skeletal symbolic situation wherein the dialogue, diction, and imagery are poised so as to cast doubt on the awareness or honesty of all the characters, to allow for a high road of ethical or a low road of psychoanalytical interpretation (as for instance R. P. Blackmur takes the upper laudatory, Maxwell Geismar the lower depreciatory). Maggie wants to be assured of the impossible, to know absolutely that there is, was, and will be no spiritual duplicity on the part of her husband, while feeling that if she doubts him at all, she has "nothing." Charlotte wants only not to be shut out of the Prince's mind—if she has but a corner she has "everything."

James represents such unsure moorings of these "vessels of consciousness" by (1) highly artificial dialogue wherein all the characters are masters of paradox and ambiguity; (2) apparent summations by a shadowy narrator which are not summations at all, but partial paraphrases of the unstable attitudes of characters who do not know what they know (Fanny Assingham is classic, continually positive and yet continually contradictory, her function apparently choric yet thoroughly untrustworthy as a reader's guide to the characters); and (3) imagery which, whether it be renderings of the character's imagination or of the narrator's (and we are rarely sure), represents no final truths about the characters but rather the shifts of their emotional attitudes. These techniques to achieve ambivalence of attitude—in dialogue, statement, and imagery— have been subjected to critical analysis many times.[2] I wish primarily here to consider the dubiousness of another of James's techniques to gain ambivalence, that is, (4) the keeping of the reader in a mist concerning the facts of the root situation of the novel, the "adultery."

One cannot be sure of the truths of the conscious and unconscious motives of others or even oneself, but one may know of facts of physical occurrence. Maggie at the end of the book is without the knowledge of whether there was in fact in the relations of her husband and Charlotte a physical adultery as well as some sort of mental one. James goes to infinite pains to straddle the question, allowing us to think as we will. I feel that the dominant impulse in James is to intimate that there never was intercourse between the two *"sposi."* Some of the critics of *The Golden Bowl* take this position, others admit to confusion concerning the facts, others consider it patent that there was a physical adultery.[3] But whatever, the impulse in James to withhold fact concerning action is quite a different thing from his leaving us in a quandary as to motive concerning action. The truth about the physical fact can make an enormous difference in the evaluating of a character or of a subtle ethical situation. To practice legerdemain with facts simply convinces the reader that the author is artificially adding mystification to life's mysteries.

Such a feeling cannot help but hurt the reader's faith in the complex world of the psyche James does render. Maggie indeed bears the entire burden of knowing nothing absolutely— it is part of the price for having, or better, believing in everything. But it is the fallacy of imitative form that we must bear

the same burden as Maggie (indeed, it is more probable that
we will not). We can know the facts of her husband's relation
with Charlotte and not destroy any equilibrium in our lives
while poignantly feeling how it is to be Maggie nobly, tragically, wanting and not wanting to know. To leave the facts of
the situation vague to the reader is simply unnecessary and,
worse, self-defeating in that the reader finds wearying the
extreme choices of both Amerigo and Maggie as either devil or
angel.

To trace this vagueness: Early in the book (chapter 4) Fanny
Assingham (such a name) believes (and we never really have
reason to doubt it) that there was no "sin" in Rome:

> Her husband again, for a little, smoked in silence. "What in the
> world, between them, ever took place?"
> "Between Charlotte and the Prince? Why, nothing—except
> their having to recognize that nothing could. That was their little
> romance—it was even their little tragedy."
> "But what the deuce did they do?"
> "Do? They fell in love with each other—but, seeing it wasn't
> possible, gave each other up."
> . . . "Didn't *he*," the Colonel inquired, "want anything more?
> Or didn't, for that matter, poor Charlotte herself?"
> She kept her eyes on him; there was a manner in it that half
> answered. "They were thoroughly in love. She might have been
> his—" She checked herself; she even for a minute lost herself.
> "She might have been anything she liked—except his wife."
> "But she wasn't," said the Colonel very smokingly.
> "She wasn't," Mrs. Assingham echoed.
> The echo, not loud but deep, filled for a little the room. He
> seemed to listen to it die away; then he began again. "How are
> you sure?"
> She waited before saying, but when she spoke it was definite.
> "There wasn't time." (Pp. 49–50.)

One might want to consider such passages as Jamesian decoys,
but the intimations of the passages are strengthened by the
consistent tone in which Amerigo is presented (or presents
himself, as you will). He impresses as a very earnest and
morally punctilious sort of *galantuomo*. For him "making love"

to twenty women, being "intimate" with them, seems to mean secret teas and shopping on back streets. So intertwined are what appear to be the thoughts of the Prince with that dubious voice of the narrator in passage after passage that we come to feel that a man who thinks thus cannot be a Casanova. Here Charlotte had asked his aid in shopping for a present for Maggie:

> There had been something, frankly, a little disconcerting in such an appeal at such an hour, on the very eve of his nuptials: it was one thing to have met the girl casually at Mrs. Assingham's and another to arrange with her thus for a morning practically as private as their old mornings in Rome and practically not less intimate. (P. 66)

With such diction we cannot help feeling that the old mornings in Rome were hardly very intimate. We cannot help feeling too that James cannot bring himself to language more definite, less ambiguous, because of some fundamental hesitation, inhibition, in his own personality concerning, to use Philip Weinstein's phrase, "passion and intimacy," or Stephen Spender's, "the physical fact of love".[4]

Amerigo will not allow a cracked bowl to be given him, as it would be a bad omen for his marriage. When questioned later by his wife as to the propriety of that secret shopping trip so close to their marriage he protests "You've never been more sacred to me than you were at that hour" (p. 430). Such an extreme answer forces us to choose between whether the Prince is being very dishonest or whether he is saying just what he felt. To be suspended between such diametrically opposed alternative choices of motive is dismaying for the reader. If we knew whether or not a physical act of adultery had occurred, we could make some sort of an ethical appraisal of the situation. There is no doubt that the Prince has been much attracted to Charlotte and that this attraction is the basis for a drama concerning a battle for control of mind, body, and spirit. But there is an immense ethical distance between a fine renunciation of physical consummation of an attraction and a Fall which is rather nauseatingly covered over by hyperbolic protestations of loyalty, by cunning equivocations, and by ambiguous gestures:

> . . . yet if her sense hadn't been absolutely closed to the possibility in him of any thought of wounding her, she might have taken his undisturbed manner, the perfection of his appearance of having recovered himself, for one of those intentions of high imperti- nence by the aid of which great people, *les grands seigneurs*, persons of her husband's class and type, always know how to reestablish a violated order. (P. 443)

The passage is unfair to Amerigo if in fact he has been conti- nent; it is unfair to the reader in the variety of alternatives it so insinuatingly implies—unfair when the merest fact could quash or confirm the insinuations.

Since we must live only with insinuations, let us look at the impressive circumstantial evidence that the Prince *has* been continent, that when he faces his wife and says to her at the moment of reconciliation, "If ever a man, since the beginning of time, acted in good faith . . ." (p. 535), he is not an outra- geous equivocator.

James never gives Amerigo and Charlotte any *time* for ex- tramarital affairs. They are always being "watched" by their mates or by their society—except for the weekend at Matchem (such another name!). But note the situation at Matchem the day before departure. The Prince is enjoying himself:

> . . . and all the more that Mrs. Verver was at hand to exchange ideas and impressions with. (P. 235)

But there are problems:

> Being thrust, systematically, with another woman, and a woman one happened, by the same token, exceedingly to like, and being so thrust that the theory of it seemed to publish one as idiotic or incapable—this was a predicament of which the dignity depended all on one's own handling. What was supremely grotesque in fact, was the essential opposition of theories—as if a galantuomo, as he at least constitutionally conceived galantuomini, could do any-

thing but blush to "go about" at such a rate with such a person as Mrs. Verver in a state of childlike innocence, the state of our primitive parents before the Fall. (P. 238)

Here at last they were free to gratify their physical and spiritual longings (they had kissed previously, but as a seal to their pledge to maintain the status quo. They live then in the "intensity" of their "accord"):

> Above all, here for the snatched instants, they could breathe so near to each other that the interval was almost engulfed in it, and the intensity both of the union and the caution became a workable substitute for contact. They had prolongations of instants that counted as visions of bliss; they had slow approximations that counted as long caresses. (P. 241)

But the affair never goes beyond the visions:

> It wasn't that, at Matchem, anything particular, anything monstrous, anything that had to be noticed permitted itself, as they said, to "happen"; there were only odd moments when the breath of the day, as it has been called, struck him so full in the face that he broke out with all the hilarity of "What indeed would *they* have made of it?" "They," were of course Maggie and her father, moping—so far as they ever consented to mope—in monotonous Eaton Square . . . . (P. 237)

Matchem is full up that night but everybody clears out in the morning except our pair, who are excited over

> the truth that the occasion constituted by the last few days couldn't possibly, save by some poverty of their own, refuse them some still other and still greater beauty. (P. 246)

Which turns out to be a short tour of Gloucester:

> "We must see the old king; we must 'do' the cathedral," he said; "we must know all about it. If we could but take," he exhaled, "the full opportunity!" And then while, for all they seemed to give him, he sounded again her eyes: "I feel the day like a great gold cup that we must somehow drain together." (P. 255)

Titillation is saved for the chapter's end, where the ambiguity between "knowing" and "doing" "everything" is again poised, as Charlotte says:

> "Ah, for things I mayn't want to know, I promise you shall find me stupid." They had reached their door, where she herself paused to explain. "These days, yesterday, last night, this morning, I've wanted everything."
>
> Well, it was all right. "You shall *have* everything." (P. 258)

It is not in the cards that she will have much, for if anything at all, the affair is but for a morning (do they "do" the cathedral?). Immediately upon return to Maggie, Amerigo learns from her lips the anguish in her past months of doubting him. She confesses her passionate need of him, and the prose would have us believe that he, at that moment, returns to her in spirit:

> . . . at the end of a moment, he had taken in what he needed to take—that his wife was *testifying*, that she adored and missed and desired him. "After all, after all," since she put it so, she was right. That was what he had to respond to; that was what, from the moment, as has been said, he "saw," he had to treat as the most pertinent thing possible. He held her close and long, in expression of their personal reunion—this, obviously, was one way of doing so. (P. 300)

Whatever equivocation one may find in the prose of the passage—whether one feels the lines are James's or paraphrase of the Prince's views or a bit of both—the overwhelming impression created by the prose here in the chapters which follow is that with Maggie watching, waiting, and manipulating, and Amerigo truly ashamed for whatever he's done or felt, he does not (would not?) "make love" in any sense to Charlotte anymore. The rest of the novel is a tracing of the psychological effects of Maggie's here asserting herself: the Prince coming home after straying, Charlotte being shut out of the house of his attention, the Princess closing the curtains on the outside psychological darkness.

The rest of the book focuses on the point of view of the Princess as she fights her own inward fight against shock and loss of faith. The rendering of this mental struggle is often admirable, but again James's coyness as to the facts of the situation causes readers to see her, as with Amerigo, as either angel or devil, or to live in an unhealthy suspension both ethically and aesthetically between the two opinions.

First the fine Maggie. She is shocked at the very possibility of duplicity in her husband, of his having "two relations with Charlotte," or of finding "evil seated . . . where she had only dreamed of good." She wishes beyond anything that Fanny Assingham might "denounce" and "revile" her for her suspicions. She says to Fanny that "if, conscientiously, you can put me in my place for a low-minded little pig . . . . I think I shall be saved." And later with Fanny, Maggie insists "I know nothing. If I did—!" "Well, if you did?" Fanny asks; Maggie replies, "I should die." She wins out against her fears of the horrors of darkness and evil by a conscious effort of the will and the imagination, by, tragically and profoundly, stifling the desire to "know":

> She didn't know why, but her time at the Museum, oddly, had done it; it was as if she hadn't come into so many noble and beautiful associations, nor secured them also for her boy, secured them even for her father, only to see them turn to vanity and doubt, turn possibly to something still worse. "I believed in him again as much as ever, and I felt how I believed in him," she said with bright, fixed eyes; "I felt it in the streets as I walked along, and it was as if that helped me and lifted me up, my being off by myself there, not having, for the moment, to wonder and watch; having, on the contrary, almost nothing on my mind." (P. 400)

And there is yet a further twist on the significance of "knowing" to come. For when she tells her husband that he knows she's ceased not to know, he says "I know nothing but what you tell me!" She answers "Then I've told you all I intended. Find out the rest—!" The reversal of roles is startling and the effect is to make Maggie awesome, magnificent, and admirable—she seems to know of things far more important than the knowledge of facts. But yet we are not sure she knows whatever she thinks she knows, or wants to know, or that we know what James would have us think.

And there are in fact (as many critics rush to point out) apparent intimations in the last hundred pages of the book of a paranoid schemer or a masochistic fantasist in the Maggie who knows and dominates, contrives and triumphs (the sort of woman Edmund Wilson finds in the governess of *The Turn of the Screw* and in other places in the late James). Such an impression on the reader's part is a natural extension of equivocal imagery and dialogue when a simple situation is not made clear.

The problem is fundamental in the late James. One critic, for example, studies the iterative imagery of *The Turn of the Screw*, and finds it rife with the Christian vocabulary of damnation vs. salvation, and so constructs a great war of good and evil. But then it must be realized that the imagery, the vocabulary, are the governess's, not James's. The whole may be seen, then, as other critics see it, as an unbalanced woman's self-dramatized world where all is battle, advantage, triumph, and loss, where she is necessarily and constantly laying plots, being spied upon, pushed into corners, suffering the infidelities, the unbelievably abrupt changes in loyalties, of people who never can be trusted, where instant decisions must be made and never doubted—in short, the "caged" woman—the paranoid—nourished on a religion of fear and sentimental romance and then starved by isolation.

Who is to say, turning to *The Golden Bowl*, with the following passages taken in isolation, whether Maggie is in the one a masochist and in the other a paranoid, or if they represent James's acute sense of the truth and honesty of the situation, or if a bit of both is true:

> (1) It all left her, as she wandered off, with the strangest of impressions—the sense, forced upon her as never yet, of an appeal, a positive confidence, from the four pairs of eyes, that was deeper than any negation, and that seemed to speak on the part of each, of some relation to be contrived by her, a relation with herself, which would spare the individual the

danger, the actual present strain, of the relation with the others. They thus tacitly put it upon her to be disposed of, the whole complexity of their peril, and she promptly saw why: because she was there, and there just as she was, to lift it off them and take it (P. 453)

(2) She saw, round about her, through the chinks of the shutters, the hard glare of nature—saw Charlotte, somewhere in it, virtually at bay, and yet denied the last grace of any protecting truth. (P. 503)

James often gives us, as here, our pick between a body of religious imagery (Maggie as savior) or one of animal imagery, (Charlotte as caged vixen) with which to interpret the situation.

What is needed are the actual facts of the situation so as to allow the reader to judge how much he feels Maggie is forgiving and how much she is fantasizing. It would be admirable, indeed divine, that Maggie learn to live with her doubts and forgive all, admirable and divine *if* she has in fact been deeply sinned against. But if we, as readers, are to keep our faith in Amerigo *and* our faith in the Princess, we must postulate an actual situation much less extreme than those the book in places intimates. The effect of these extreme and unpleasant choices occurs by a withholding of simple evidence, and the effect is quite damaging in that the reader can lose faith in the book's continuity of ethical attitude, and in James's own complete control of the situation as an artist, and feel that personal failings of James have come into play.

I find this withholding—for whatever reason—sad in Henry James, a failing in such an acute and penetrating spirit. He could have done without it. The best James creates symbolic situations within which pain is unavoidable and inexorable. The symbolic situations are those which rack all human lives, as for instance in the triangle of *The Ambassadors*: a young man, a woman approaching middle age, and Strether getting old. The appeal of each to the other is obvious, as are also the small duplicities, the considerable nobilities achieved, and the difficult renunciations necessary. Four people are on a rack in *The Golden Bowl*. A father and a daughter love each other and cannot bear to part. Amerigo has no choice but to live on love, and Charlotte hardly has that. There are no crimes in any of the relationships save those repressions which, heroically, no one allows to surface into action. They are all, in a word, decent people, neither divine nor demonic, trying hard to make their lives as "beautiful" as they can. They all seem to recognize that, in Fanny's phrase, "forms . . . are two-thirds of conduct" (p. 277). They live (as most of us do) trying to give some form to their lives—a feat of the imagination in the museum of its experiences. "Everything's terrible, cara, in the heart of man" says the Prince to the Princess, but then adds quickly of Charlotte's dark condition, "She's making her life . . . she'll make it" (p.535). This is, as I see it, the Jamesian summation. Pain is endurable. We can build our lives into somewhat of a work of art, into a Golden Bowl, out of what we must submit to.

The fear that perhaps forms may be *three-thirds* of life is too unpleasant to contemplate for very long; one must live most of the time within cherished values, whether illusions or not, rather than do so. Such is Miguel de Unamuno's explicit theme, and the implicit theme of much of modern art, including James's art. James's characters make their accommodations, but James has seemed to many recent critics to be wanting to keep the reader from doing so:

> The horror of this book—and its genius—is that it sustains a twofold vision to the very end and insists upon the interplay of diametrically opposed modes of understanding the same events.
> There are few events that are not susceptible of two interpretations; the duality is omnipresent and unrelenting. (Sallie Sears, *The Negative Imagination*, p. 173)

I think the description is correct, but not the evaluation—that is, of the "genius" of the book being a function of the reader's suspension between diametrically opposed modes of seeing. In so far as the formulation is accurate it points up the ethical discontinuity that is in the book. We, the readers, should not be so suspended in bewilderment, though the characters might well be.

Sears later speaks of the novel as morally "absurd":

Moreover, in a certain sense the absurdity is the whole point, for it is precisely the arbitrary reign of consciousness that James's work celebrates: the capacity of human mind to establish new conventions, change the significance of words, cut down its "prior term," make and unmake meanings, both reflecting and creating itself in its supreme fictions. (P.222)

The final term is of course Stevens's, out of Vaihinger, and the passage is but one demonstration that contemporary criticism is coming to find the ambience of the idea of illusion as value congenial, at least for James:

Many lies have had to be told to save the marriage, but they have been, as in *The Wings of the Dove* and *The Ambassadors*, "constructive" lies—the lies by which civilization can be held together. The whole truth, James suggests, could destroy civilization, for everything, as the Prince is made to say, is "terrible in the heart of man." All the more reason, this novel seems to imply, that the terrors of the heart should not be translated into life. They would be unbearable. James had felt, in his early days in Rome, that the dead past must be kept buried; the primitive, uncovered, was too dangerous to continuation of life. So in the last of his "philosophical" novels he places himself on the side of the "illusions" by which man lives. Like Marlow, in Conrad's "Heart of Darkness," James's characters tell lies because the truth can serve no useful purpose. Certain lies can be extremely useful. (Leon Edel, *Henry James*, 5:215)

The story of all four is a narrative of perplexed, fallible human beings whose relationships at the beginning are superficially as perfect as the seemingly flawless gold-covered crystal bowl, but which, like the bowl, possess a hidden crack. Like the bowl, their world must be recognized for what it is. Like the bowl, it will split into fragments which by themselves are meaningless, but which by a supreme effort of imagination can be fitted together again into a thing of beauty which all four will have helped to create, and which they must henceforth work together to maintain. (W. F. Wright, *The Madness of Art*, p. 244)

I prefer Wright's formulation. "Lies" is too banal a word for the Jamesian context. There is a certain amount of overstatement in Edel's "lies" here, in Sear's "absurdity" above, and in much of the commentary concerning James's aestheticism in dealing with "how to live, what to do," as if the "will to believe" were somehow low and unworthy. We ought to be past that now.

William James refined the terms of the debate between "science" and the "will," "truth" and "beauty" in his "The Will To Believe" and other of his essays; Henry James did much the same in his symbolic situations. It is not the aesthetic or ethic of illusion as value that causes the limitations in *The Golden Bowl*. Rather it is some personal hesitations which reveal themselves in aesthetic and ethical equivocations. These do not impress this reader as complex, but as disruptive, staining a masterful art with the now-you-see it, now-you-don't of the shell game.

Notes

1. On "Aesthetic Shock" see my *The Rape of Cinderella*, Chapter 1.

2. Critics that tend to focus, whether in praise or blame, on James's techniques for ambiguity are (1) Edmund Wilson, *The Triple Thinkers* (New York, 1938), (2) Marius Bewley, *The Complex Fate* (New York, 1967), (3) Frederick Crews, *The Tragedy of Manners* (New Haven, 1958), (4) Dorothea Krook, *The Ordeal of Consciousness in Henry James* (Cambridge, 1962), (5) Sallie Sears, *The Negative Imagination* (Ithaca, N.Y., 1968), (6) Charles Samuels, *The Ambiguity of Henry James* (Champaign, Ill., 1971), (7) J. A. Ward, "The Ambiguities of Henry James," *Sewanee Review* (1975), (8) Philip Weinstein, *Henry James and The Requirements of the Imagination* (Cambridge, Mass., 1971).

3. Consider these opinions:

(1) "Mr. Blackmur has Charlotte and the Prince lovers from their meeting in Rome, but it seems quite clear that their relation was not consummated until the Matchem weekend" (Arthur Mizener, in *The New Republic*, 18 August 1952).

(2) "Before the pair of marriages took place we are made to understand that an undefinedly intimate relation had existed between the Prince and Charlotte, of which Maggie and her father were unaware; and after the marriages we are made to under-

stand that the undefinedly intimate relation was resumed "(Stuart P. Sherman, in *The Question of Henry James*, ed. F. Dupee [New York, 1945], p. 88).

(3) "The matter of the innocence or guilt of Prince Amerigo and Charlotte Stant is of first importance in any present attempt to interpret or to evaluate *The Golden Bowl*. . . . Standing opposed to those who accept the adulterous relationship in the novel is Jean Kimball, who argues that the illicit alliance is entirely fictive and that Charlotte Stant is the innocent victim of Maggie Verver's viciousness. . . . Kimball's orient discovery not only permits a point of departure for a closer view of many of the more or less enigmatic situations in the novel, but opens upon the definite possibility for a broader interpretation of the work as a whole" (J. A. Clair, *The Ironic Dimension in the Fiction of Henry James* [1965], pp. 80–82. The Kimball essay is in *American Literature* 28 [1957]: 449–68).

(4) "We must remember that Charlotte initially renounced thoughts of marriage with the Prince because they lacked money, that she marries Adam after he has told her that he needs her for the sake of Maggie, and that she continues to share secrets with the Prince, even to taking with him an unchaperoned excursion which, whether or not it involves physical adultery—a point on which James is deliberately obscure—most certainly amounts to deception of Maggie and Adam" (W. F. Wright, *The Madness of Art* [Lincoln, Nebr., 1962], p. 248).

(5) "To preserve our sanity as readers we must of course resort to a kind of critical Occam's razor here must assume that the mystery which Maggie so painfully uncovers is at least a genuine sexual betrayal and not the even more mysterious pretense of one . . . the need, if one is to survive, of creating one's facts and of choosing to act on one's own fictions" (Ruth Bernard Yeazell, *Language and Knowledge in the Late Novels of Henry James* [Chicago, 1976], pp. 3, 99).

Mildred Hartsock attempts to summarize opinion on this issue and others in her "Unintentional Fallacy: Critics and The Golden Bowl," *Modern Language Quarterly* 35 (1974): 272–88.

4. See Leon Edel, *Henry James: The Master* (Philadelphia, 1972), pp. 222–23, 407; and Philip Weinstein, *Henry James and the Requirements of the Imagination* (Cambridge, Mass., 1971), pp. 193–94.

7
Contextualism in Art and Life: Social Criticism

The foregoing chapters have disposed themselves about various metacritical ideas, primarily those of "illusion as value" and of "exultant dualism" as they find expression in some texts in English and American literature since the Romantic movement. I want now to consider in the chapters remaining various ramifications not only of these two ideas but also of the theism sketched out in chapter 1 in areas of meditation beyond the literary. A metacritical idea impels, of course, correlative attitudes toward art and life in the areas of criticism, ethics, sociology, and religion, attitudes which may provide a basis for somewhat of a common approach to areas so often and largely ensconced in their own terms. It is the idea of the fundamental need for continuity in aesthetic, social, and personal contexts that may link these areas, while preserving the distinction between criticism and metacriticism in each.

The idea of illusion as value as I have presented it in chapters 1 and 2 flows from two insights into, or reactions to, experience, one negative and one positive. One, negative, "skeptical," that to the reason truth or absolutes cannot be known, values cannot be proved, and that this tragic condition of life can not essentially change. The other, positive, "idealistic," that the will should not, cannot, accept the reason's findings, that even in the absence of faith the instinct for self-preservation alone demands imaginative orders, assumptions, or illusions of permanence and value. Nietzsche expresses the resultant dualistic dilemma:

in order that there might be some degree of consciousness in the world, an unreal world of error had to arise: beings with a belief in permanency, in individuals, etc. Not until an imaginary world, in contradiction to the absolute flux, had arisen, was it possible to erect on this foundation a structure of knowledge; and now finally we can see the fundamental error [the belief in permanence] upon which everything else rests. . . . but this error can only be destroyed with life itself. . . . our organs are adjusted to error. . . . the fact that we know that we err does not do away with error. And that is not a bitter thought! We must love and cultivate error: it is the mother of knowledge. (Hans Vaihinger, *The Philosophy of "As If,"* pp. 346–47, quoted from Nietzsche's *Werke*, vol. 12, p. 46)

For "error" read serially "illusion" or "fiction," "ideals," or even "faith," to see how consonant this articulation may be with many others in modern art and thought. Consider, for the purposes of this chapter, the following passages of a few of the more noted early "relativists" in comparative sociology:

Finally, Pareto [1848–1923] implies a kind of inherent contradiction between scientific truth and social utility. According to him, the truth about society is something of a factor in social breakdown. If this contradiction is authentic, if the true is not the useful, if the useful consists of fictions or illusions, then everyone is free to choose truth in terms of personal preference, or utility in terms of the society to which he belongs. (Raymond Aron, *Main Currents in Sociological Thought*, vol. 2, pp. 169–70 [Chap. 7, "Final Remarks on Pareto"])

The modern peoples have made morals and morality a separate domain, by the side of religion, philosophy, and politics. In that sense, morals is an impossible and unreal category. It has no existence, and can have none. The word "moral" means what belongs or appertains to the mores. Therefore the category of morals can never be defined without reference to something outside of itself. Ethics, having lost connection with the ethos of a people, is an attempt to systematize the current notions of right and wrong upon some basic principle, generally with the purpose of establishing morals on an absolute doctrine, so that it shall be universal, absolute, and everlasting. In a general way also, whenever a thing can be called moral, or connected with some ethical generality, it is thought to be "raised," and disputants whose method is to employ ethical generalities assume especial authority for themselves and their views. These methods of discussion are most employed in treating of social topics, and they are disastrous to sound study of facts. They help to hold the social sciences under the dominion of metaphysics. (William Graham Sumner [1840–1910], *Folkways*, p. 37 [first published in 1906])

The sophisticated modern temper has made of social relativity, even in the small area which it has recognized, a doctrine of despair. It has pointed out its incongruity with the orthodox dreams of permanence and ideality and with the individual's illusions of autonomy. It has argued that if human experience must give up these, the nutshell of existence is empty. But to interpret our dilemma in these terms is to be guilty of an anachronism. It is only the inevitable cultural lag that makes us insist that the old must be discovered again in the new, that there is no solution but to find the old certainty and stability in the new plasticity. The recognition of cultural relativity carries with it its own values, which need not be those of the absolutist philosophies. (Ruth Benedict [1887–1948] *Patterns of Culture*, p. 278 [first published in 1934])

There is something a bit off-putting in the tone of all three of these formulations; Pareto perhaps too jaundiced, Sumner too arrogant, Benedict too sanguine concerning man's need for absolutes. All lack something of the tragic and the absurdist tone of Nietzsche, or of the poets of chapter 2 with their images of chairs in the sky, playhouses, daffodils in the Milky Way, greeny flowers, god-sleight "out of nothing," their chants for "our proper dark," for "ceremonies of innocence" and the "artifice of eternity" (or, to be sure, of James's sense of life as "two-thirds form"). But they are all three facing the dilemma, not turning their backs to it, as happens in much sociological literature.

To repeat the position of chapter 2 (a position that I think finds very little dissent): the full existential experience of the modern human dilemma, as outlined by Nietzsche, is to be found in the creative arts of a given culture. It is therefore a possibility worth considering that the accuracy of response and precision of articulation in sociological criticism may be helped by the methodologies of aesthetic analysis and literary criticism.

The trouble is that much of what goes under the name of criticism in the arts is in fact either scholarship or metacriticism. Criticism is the close analysis and articulation of the "tone"—the dominant attitudes—and continuity of tone of a unique context. Scholarship is the gathering of all information necessary to perform the critical act, and metacriticism is the comparing of one unique context with another or with any other outside (i.e., not intrinsic to the given context) standard of valuation. There is, I think, something to be gained from trying to define what constitutes a true critical analysis of a unique given social context in terms similar to those I have used for defining a true critical analysis of a unique given aesthetic context.

Ruth Benedict, we are told by Margaret Mead in a preface to Benedict's *Patterns of Culture*, was originally a student of literature, and her anthropological investigations convinced her that

> if one took these cultures whole—the religion, the mythology, the everyday ways of man and women—then the internal consistency and the intricacy was as aesthetically satisfying to the would-be explorer as was any single work of art. (P. ix)

Benedict's concluding chapters indeed do seem to me to embody a rare and successful application of sound critical principles to cultural contexts. The "configuration" of a social context is her term for what I have called the unique "tone" of a given literary context:

> Nor are these configurations we have discussed "types" in the sense that they represent a fixed constellation of traits. Each one is an empirical characterization, and probably is not duplicated in its entirety anywhere else in the world. Nothing could be more unfortunate than an effort to characterize all cultures as exponents of a limited number of fixed and selected types. Categories be-

come a liability when they are taken as inevitable and applicable alike to all civilizations and all events. . . .

. . . There is no "law," but several different characteristic courses which a dominant attitude may take. . . . There is always the possibility that the description of the culture is disoriented rather than the culture itself. Then again, the nature of the integration may be merely outside our experience and difficult to perceive. When these difficulties have been removed, the former by better fieldwork, the latter by more acute analysis, the importance of the integration of cultures may be even clearer than it is today. Nevertheless it is important to recognize the fact that not all cultures are by any means the homogeneous structures we have described for Zuni and the Kwakiutl. It would be absurd to cut every culture down to the Procrustean bed of some catchword characterization. The danger of lopping off important facts that do not illustrate the main proposition is grave enough even at best. It is indefensible to set out upon an operation that mutilates the subject and erects additional obstacles against our eventual understanding of it. (Pp. 228, 238)

A focus on "internal consistency," "intricacy," and uniqueness of context and tone; accuracy in observation of significant detail and precision of analysis and articulation of unique "configuration" before any attempts at "integration"; and, finally, the distrust of "types" and "categories" (for which see below, chapter 8)—these are the enduring qualities of good scholarship and good criticism.

Sumner's term for the customs which proceed from specific social attitudes—from Benedict's "configurations"—is the "folkways":

The structure thus built up is not physical, but societal and institutional, that is to say, it belongs to a category which must be defined and studied by itself. It is a category in which custom produces continuity, coherence, and consistency, so that the word "structure" may properly be applied to the fabric of relations and prescribed positions with which societal functions are permanently connected. The process of making folkways is never superseded or changed. It goes on now just as it did at the beginning of civilization. (*Folkways*, p. 35)

It is thus the sociologist's job to probe, analyze, and articulate the unique folkways of a unique social context caught in a unique moment in the flow of time and change. Pareto's concept of "residues"—the actual attitudes which impel given social behavior in a given context—is not very far from Benedict's "configurations" or Sumner's "folkways," and the true business of sociology for Pareto is likewise the analysis and articulation of the residues of a culture. One could also mention in this context Emile Durkheim's concept of the "*conscience collective*," the unique manifestations of which in unique social action constitute in his terms the business of sociological study. The art critic probes for the true tonality of the aesthetic context, the social critic for the true tonality of the social context. The ultimate aim of the critic is the precise articulation of the unique tonality.

Just as in the literature on art, what is in fact apparent in a survey of the literature of social contexts is the usual confusing of the mental operations scholarship, criticism, and metacriticism. One may do sloppy and inaccurate data gathering, or do it rather well, but then rest with such, pretending it to be sound social analysis or criticism. One may do the scholarship poorly or well, and then exhibit very little skill in sensing the continuities of central attitudes (or "tone" or "configuration") in the given society, continuities which may or may not be implicit in the data collected. Finally, and as usually happens, one may have metacritical predilections, preconceptions concerning sociology, psychology, politics, economics, history, religion, what you will, that one cannot keep from predisposing one's analysis of social context. One's ultimate metacritical positions need not, ought not, hinder accurate and precise social scholarship and criticism, though they usually do. For all the brilliance in say, Sumner's exhibition of the relativity of social values in his *Folkways*, his dislike for metaphysics causes him to slight the other side of the equation of the human dilemma: man's need for values in which he can believe with some absoluteness.

It is this other side of the equation, the response to experience of those whose thought touches on the metacritical need for faith, that deepens and enriches what seems to me the better sociological criticism of our time:

> The substance of all religion is . . . deeply rooted in human life; it grows out of the necessities of life. In other words, religion fulfils a definite cultural function in every human society. This is not a platitude. It contains a scientific refutation of the repeated attacks on religion by the less enlightened rationalists. If religion is indispensable to the integration of the community, just because it satisfies spiritual needs by giving man certain truths and teaching him how to use these truths, then it is impossible to regard religion as a trickery, as an "opiate for the masses," as an invention of priests, capitalists, or any other servants of vested interests.
>
> . . . Let us work for the maintenance of the eternal truths which have guided mankind out of barbarism to culture, and the loss of which seems to threaten us with barbarism again. The rationalist and agnostic must admit that even if he himself cannot accept these truths, he must at least recognize them as indispensable pragmatic figments without which civilization cannot exist. (Bronislaw Malinowski, "On the Social Functions of Religion," in *Theories of Society*, vol. 2, pp. 1094–95 [reprinted from *Foundations of Faith and Morals*, 1936])

> Any religion, while it lasts, and on its own level, gives an apparent meaning to life, provides the framework for a culture, and protects the mass of humanity from boredom and despair. (T. S. Eliot, *Notes towards the Definition of Culture*, p.106)

> But though history may be capable either of assisting or of paralysing new religious experiences, it can never manage to abolish the need for religious experience. (Mircea Eliade "Conclusions," in *Patterns in Comparative Religion*, pp.464–65)

All three of these important voices in twentieth-century thought are theists of one sort or another. All focus however, at least here, on simple need for faith, belief, values, or at the very least for "indispensable pragmatic figments." A fourth voice:

To believe in God is to long for His existence and, further, it is

to act as if He existed: it is to live by this longing and to make it
the inner spring of our action. This longing or hunger for divinity
begets hope, hope begets faith, and faith and hope beget charity.
Of this divine longing is born our sense of beauty, of finality, of
goodness. (Miguel de Unamuno, *The Tragic Sense of Life*, pp. 184–
85 [first published in 1921])

But I have jumped too far too quickly; perhaps most readers
are not willing to go so far at this point, or at any point. There
are, however, wide areas of possible agreement on methodology and approach before one need part ways down separate
metacritical paths.

Benedict speaks of the "integration of a culture,"
Malinowski of the "integration of the community," both rec-
ognizing the simple necessity for order, coherence, and continuity upon which much mental and psychic activity may
rest. Durkheim's analysis of man's *anomie*, of man in a
nineteenth-century industrial landscape without a satisfying
social context, living a life without meaningful continuity or
significant coherence, man bewildered or lost in a chaotic and
painful existence, is an anticipation of Eliot's Waste Land in a
twentieth-century urban landscape. Eliot's sense is that man
lives in boredom or despair if he lives deprived of a sense of
belonging to some sort of order, *communitas*, or vital context.
Charles Horton Cooley asserts that the individual self is in
good measure *defined* by the richness or poverty of the immediate social context in which he has found himself:

the view here maintained is that human nature is not something
existing separately in the individual. . . . It is the nature which is
developed and expressed in those simple, face-to-face groups that
are somewhat alike in all societies; groups of the family, the play-
ground, and the neighborhood. In the essential similarity of these
is to be found the basis, in experience, for similar ideas and sentiments in the human mind. In these, everywhere, human nature
comes into existence. Man does not have it at birth; he cannot
acquire it except through fellowship, and it decays in isolation.

What else can human nature be than a trait of primary groups?
Surely not an attribute of the separate individual—supposing
there were any such thing—since its typical characteristics, such

as affection, ambition, vanity, and resentment, are inconceivable apart from society. If it belongs, then, to man in association, what kind or degree of association is required to develop it? Evidently nothing elaborate, because elaborate phases of society are transient and diverse while human nature is comparatively stable and universal. In short the family and neighborhood life is essential to its genesis and nothing more is.

. . . We must see and feel the communal life of family and local groups as immediate facts, not as combinations of something else. And perhaps we shall do this best by recalling our own experience and extending it through sympathetic observation. (Charles Horton Cooley, *Social Organization*, pp. 29–31)

Cooley's view reinforces what my experience in life and literature has taught me. As one moves from family to clan, to village, to country, and finally to a sense of internationalism, the passional ties become more and more vaporous, less and less subjectively meaningful, valuable, or loved. The possibility of living within a graceful, harmonious whole, consonant in all of its parts, diminishes with the increasing complexity of the diverse elements within the whole. The relativity, the purely "normative" nature of the values cherished within a given social context may be clear in the objective comparison of different contexts, but no less clear should be the necessity for coherence and continuity of those values within a given context, for a harmony which can seem absolute *enough* to the large part of the citizenry in that local social context.

The social critic must evaluate a given social context not by the values he brings extrinsically to the study, but in terms of the continuity and coherence of the values that have developed within, that is, are intrinsic to, that context. He may later judge that context on a scale of metacritical value personal to him or to the group to which he belongs, but he will not then be a social critic, but a metacritical advocate, aware of and hopefully honest about doing something different. Being a social critic and being a citizen of a given society are likewise different actions; both are laudable, but the confusion of the two processes, compounded with a strong dose of arrogance, is an all-too-familiar observed condition:

We can also learn to respect every other culture as a whole, however inferior to our own it may appear, or however justly we may disapprove of some features of it: the deliberate destruction of another culture as a whole is an irreparable wrong, almost as evil as to treat human beings like animals. (T. S. Eliot, *Notes towards the Definition of Culture*, pp. 139–40.

The true social critic will have Keats's "negative capability," that is, the ability to empathize with the mores, the folkways, the configurations, the tone of the culture he is investigating, to feel its rhythms, its continuities, its beauties (however meager they may seem to be), to assess whether the culture does in fact provide some depth, richness, sense of joy in belonging, to the large majority of its citizens, and then to articulate these assessments. The process repeated with other social cultures or contexts will breed understanding and tolerance; it will also breed some skepticism about the possibility or desirability of the achievement of millennial dreams of a one-world society where all human values would allegedly be present and all human evils excluded. It will affirm, in Eliot's terms, a love of diversity, of local particularity:

> For it must follow from what I have already pleaded about the value of local cultures, that a world culture which was simply a *uniform* culture would be no culture at all. We should have a humanity de-humanised. It would be a nightmare. But on the other hand, we cannot resign the idea of world-culture altogether. . . .
> We can only conceive it, as the logical term of relations between cultures. Just as we recognise that the parts of Britain must have in one sense, a common culture, though this common culture is only actual in diverse local manifestations, so we must aspire to a common world culture, which will yet not diminish the particularity of the constituent parts. (Ibid., p. 136)

T. S. Eliot as social critic and metacritic has come in for some hard knocks; Ezra Pound, his friend and peer, much more so. They both felt, however, that they were fighting the good fight, and, in most ways, the same fight:

Another struggle has been the struggle to keep the value of a local and particular character, of a particular culture in this awful maelstrom, this awful avalanche toward uniformity. The whole fight is for the conservation of the individual soul. ("Interview with Ezra Pound," *Paris Review* no. 28 (1962), p. 43.)

Pound in *The Cantos*:

> Earth and water dye the wind in your valley . . . .
> . . . feelings have the colour of nature. . . .
> Manners are from earth and from water
> They arise out of hills and streams
> The spirit of air is of the country
> Men's manners cannot be one
> (same, identical). . . .
> Hills and streams colour the air,
> vigour, tranquility, not one set of rules.
> Vigour, quietude, are of place . . .
> Different each, different customs
> but one root in the equities. . . .
> Ancestral spring making breed, a pattern. . . .
> & with Chou rite at the root of it
> The root is thru all of it . . . .
> One village in order,
> one valley will reach the four seas
> . . . village usage
> to see what style for the casting
> Filiality and fraternity are the root,
> Talents to be considered as branches. . . .
> Precise terminology is the first implement,
> dish and container. . . .
> Unitas Charitatis, consuetudo diversa
> [The unity of charity, the diversity of customs] . . .
> Time mother of Manors
> Nor can the King create a new custom . . .
> (Pp. 689, 698, 699, 707–11, 749, 772.)

Pound has "no dogma" but loves the local manifestations of man's need to venerate, as in the ancient Chinese rituals of *muan bpo*, or the *Li Ki*, or the Confucian vision, or in the

Eleusinian rites of ancient Greece, or a priest's first mass in a contemporary Italian village. "Art is local," "Temples, plural," "All gates are holy," are iterated motifs in the late Cantos. All of which may bring us back (see above, pp. 29 and 49) to Yeats's "Prayer for my Daughter":

> O may she live like some green laurel
> Rooted in one dear perpetual place. . . .
>
> And may her bridegroom bring her to a house
> Where all's accustomed, ceremonious;
> For arrogance and hatred are the wares
> Peddled in the thoroughfares.
> How but in custom and in ceremony
> Are innocence and beauty born?
> Ceremony's a name for the rich horn,
> And custom for the spreading laurel tree.

And back (see above, pp. 19, 56) to Simone Weil's *The Need for Roots*:

> The degree of respect owing to human collectivities is a very high one, for several reasons.
>
> To start with, each is unique, and, if destroyed, cannot be replaced. One sack of corn can always be substituted for another sack of corn. The food that collectivity supplies, for the souls of those who form part of it has no equivalent in the entire universe.
>
> Secondly, because of its continuity, a collectivity is already moving forward into the future. It contains food, not only for the souls of the living, but also for the souls of beings yet unborn which are to come into the world during the immediately succeeding centuries.
>
> Lastly, due to this same continuity, a collectivity has its roots in the past. It constitutes the sole agency for preserving the spiritual treasures accumulated by the dead, the sole transmitting agency by means of which the dead can speak to the living. . . .
>
> But it does not follow from this that collectivities are superior to human beings. . . .
>
> It very often happens that the roles are reversed. There are collectivities which, instead of serving as food, do just the opposite: they devour souls. (Pp. 8–9.)

One may label such articulations, as has often been done, as "conservative," but political labels never do for intensely realized experiences of intensely realized imaginations. Yeats, Eliot, Pound, are among the handful of great poets of our century, and to dismiss their social meditations, and those of Simone Weil, to whom they are kin in both substance and realization, as crankish or conservative will not finally diminish them. The passages breathe an awareness of the evils of collectivities, of stagnant or tyrannical societies, upon which the great majority of social and political literature has focused since the Romantic movement. But they all emphasize what needs to be emphasized: the good, the blessings, the need of vital social contexts and continuities.

Further, those blessings are for these observers primarily found there where Charles Cooley finds them, in the family, the neighborhood and region, or, if beyond, in a national or international unity based not on uniformity of culture, but on the welcome diversity of local contexts. It is there, in the local or regional context, that the citizen seems to flourish. And it is there too that the social critic can best function, where he can view the unique local context and its comprehensibility, as the critic in the arts can view the unique created aesthetic object.

In summary, the dilemma posed by Nietzsche concerning the apparent relativity of values, the impermanence of things, set against the human mind's hunger for absoluteness of values and permanence of self, is most capable of resolution at the contextual level in art and in society. Hart Crane has effectively articulated the contextualist aesthetic in poetry, and, by implication, the contextualist approach to cultures:

> It may not be possible to say that there is, strictly speaking, any "absolute" experience. But it seems evident that certain aesthetic experience (and this may for a time engross the total faculties of the spectator) can be called absolute, inasmuch as it approximates a formally convincing statement of a conception or apprehension of life that gains our unquestioning assent, and under the conditions of which our imagination is unable to suggest a further detail consistent with the design of the aesthetic whole. . . . Such a

poem is at least a stab at a truth, and to such an extent may be differentiated from other kinds of poetry and called "absolute."

. . . I found that I was really building [in *The Bridge*] a bridge between so-called classic experience and many divergent realities of our seething, confused cosmos of today, which has no formulated mythology yet for classic poetic reference or for religious exploitation. . . . Plato doesn't live today because of the intrinsic "truth" of his statements, their only living truth today consists in the "fact" of their harmonious relationship to each other. This grace is, or partakes of, poetry. (Philip Horton, *Hart Crane: The Life of an American Poet*, pp. 323, 325, 326, 343.)

The "assent" is emotional: the will's need for absolutes temporarily satisfied by the poem's contextual harmony or intrinsic grace; so with social contexts. The fact that, abstractly considered, human values seem merely relative, truth likewise, does not deny the totally engrossing hold of a context and its "mythology" upon the responsive imagination. One can for instance hardly overestimate the pull of family, village, local loves, on the human spirit that has known them. It is so in part because, as Cooley asserts, to lose one's context of local loves is to lose one's sense of oneself.

The "local" context may be of a place, there where family or friends or memories are, or it may be a place in the mind, there where a store of things loved is kept. In either case the local context provides a center, a focus, a place to come home to when the periphery, one's life beyond the local loves, however good, is not sufficient to sustain one.

The center of one's loves cannot by definition include all things worthy to love; it must of necessity be a selection from the myriad possibilities of living a good life. Hence the possibility of many different centers (that is, pluralism). Hence too the necessity of exclusion of much good from one's center. It is very hard to give up good and beautiful things to love, other graceful patterns of life, so as to hold onto one's center, but there will be no center at all if one does not do so.

Therefore the necessity for the self-imposition of imperatives in one's social and ethical being. Consistency of tone in one's life can be seen as a measure of ethical quality. As we use the word "continuity" in criticism, so we may use it in ethics. The flow of emotional logic would run something like this: One must stay loyal, faithful, to one's center to keep that center. No amount of peripheral joy can make up for the loss of continuity at the center of one's soul. One will be measured socially and ethically by the continuity of his actions, not only by others of some depth of insight, but, more importantly, by one's self. And it need not be a rational, it will more likely be an intuitive judgment, an emotional realization that one is, bit by bit, losing one's emotional center, as one engages in actions that do not form a continuum with the dreams one has chosen to be defined by:

> M'amour, m'amour
> what do I love and
> where are you?

> That I lost my center
> fighting the world.

> The dreams clash
> and are shattered—

> and that I tried to make a paradiso
> terrestre.
> (Ezra Pound, from "Canto 117")

To act out the imperatives of one's center is to be seen then not only as obligation, but privilege, since it allows keeping what "thou lovest well" as "thy true heritage" ("Canto 81"). Absolute freedom to do what one wants is clearly seen, in this context of thought, as a prison, as it will sooner or later lock a person from his center, as one dream context shatters another. If love between people is to have any continuity, it must be the love of a shared center, of a shared dream, of shared obligations. Freedom then is the opportunity, the privilege, of carrying out the obligations to what one loves. Thus it is that we can say that life without obligations is meaningless.[1]

One can assess the continuity and the quality of a social

context or the acts of an individual within that context only if one has rightly understood the nature of the shared dreams, the central attitudes, that impel the social process or the individual who is part of that context. As the literary critic must judge the work of art by the continuity, the inner harmony of both the structural principles and of the smallest details of execution in the work, so must the social critic respond both to the central attitudes toward life in the given social context and to the unique details of daily life within that context. Intuition, insight, and the artist's gift of empathy with unique context are here more necessary than data gathering, and certainly more precise than the laying over the data of precut patterns of categories of societies-in-general. It is the artist in the social or ethical critic that generates the true criticism, not the scholarship, not the metacritical position.

One cannot keep one's own metacriticism of life, one's context of values, out of the process for very long however, and sooner or later the social critic wonders if there are any criteria, other than the necessary, insufficient one of continuity, that define one culture as better than another. The question has already been considered in chapter 2, with only the broadest sorts of conclusions offered. I have little to add here, as we are in the area of clash over ultimate values, where the arguments are endless and perhaps insoluble. My position is that one context is preferable to another in so far as it exhibits, concomitant with its own core beliefs or loves, a tolerance, an understanding, a sentiment for the loveliness, the grace of other core beliefs or loves. Pound's preference for "Kung and Eleusis" ("Canto 52"), what he calls the Confucian and the Mediterranean "sanity," is largely a judgment of the measure of such sentiment in these ancient cultural contexts, contexts which in Pound's view constitute "little light[s] in a great darkness" ("Canto 116"). Matthew Arnold's more muted preference for the "Hellenic" spirit as compared to the "Hebraic," in *Culture and Anarchy*, is but one other formulation based on a similar judgment. Yet man can suffer anomie in a social anarchy, a society all periphery with no core *communitas*, just as he can suffer in a society with no periphery, all

core and arrogant monomania. One—one meaning many—
suffers least when a social context of a good measure of core
beauty and coherence tends also toward the attitudes of sentiment and tolerance: we can "settle" (define) the metacritical
issues only thus far and thus negatively. To expect more is to
turn away from the "tragic sense of life" of Unamuno, of
Santayana, of Eliot, from that metacriticism of life which
seems to this critic better, that is, more productive of grace
and sentiment, than those encompassed by the various postures of exultant, rather than tragic, dualism.

Cooley calls on the social critic to recall and extend his own
experience of family and neighborhood in order to understand
"human nature." This process will finally move the discussion
from the unique to the general ("human nature"), but it will
first bring one home to the "heart's field," to the particular,
there where most of the human drama takes place. This is the
right place to be for criticism, whether or not one is prepared
to go further metacritically with Cooley. It is indeed as I recall
and extend my own experience with family and neighborhood
that I have come to my own understanding of the human need
for continuity, the need that underlies all of the thought in this
book. I have had the blessings, as well as the turmoil, of
growing up in America in an immigrant neighborhood in up-
state New York, composed largely of Italian immigrant
families, with a few families of Lebanese Christians intermin-
gled. The "Americans" lived on the other side of town and
were largely unknown to the children of East Utica. The
vision of life which I absorbed was largely that of Mt. Lebanon, though what is common to Mediterranean peasant culture caused things Italian to blend easily into that vision.
Later, at Kenyon College in Ohio, then at Oxford University
in England, the shocks of cultural and intellectual clash made
very vivid to my imagination the realization that cultures are
fragile beauties, visions or dreams easily lost if not cherished
and maintained, and that they are precious at the same time
that they are rooted in no absolute truths that are apparent to
the rational eye.

The vision that flowed into me from home and neighborhood in East Utica was one that humanized nature, the universe, and God in terms of the Lebanese family, its garden, and its mountain village. The Father ideally rules the family, but only in the context of the worship of the Mother. Grandparents have the double respect of parents and of age. The family and the clan stand together in the village; one village tells tales about the other, one region about the other. Dogs, vegetables, fruit trees, and all natural phenomena are seen in terms of brothers, sisters, cousins. God is seen now as village patriarch, now as neighborhood visitor, even at times as village jokester; He appreciates laughter, the well-told tale, the well-made *arak*. One weeds the garden and prunes the vine not out of hated obligation, but out of love of the lettuce leaf and the grape. The apricot thirsts for the water of the spring, which the villager brings to the garden plot, and the villager's thirst is quenched by both the apricot and the spring. So too are the ideal relationships between brothers, cousins, neighbors, and strangers.[2]

This idyllic vision (attained of course only fitfully) has its unique detail in the context of the unique Lebanese village (such as, say, Gibran's lamented village, above p. 100), or in the context of a unique ethnic American neighborhood, but clearly it is also somewhat harmonious in its large outlines with central attitudes within peasant villages around the earth and throughout the past. Here then we may consider Cooley's premise: it may be that family and neighborhood experience are so fundamental to man's early evolution as social being that there has been sufficient agreement in most men's sense of self to be able to speak of the idea of a "human nature" existing beyond the relativities of given social contexts.[3] Unamuno would go further to assert that a "universal" human nature is created by the fundamental human need for continuity and fear of discontinuity, which needs and fears beget faith or hope, and, as self-pity evolves into the larger pity for the human condition, finally beget charity. Thus Unamuno's imperative:

What is our heart's truth, anti-rational though it be? The im-

mortality of the human soul, the truth of the persistence of our
consciousness without any termination whatsoever, the truth of
the human finality of the Universe. And what is its moral proof?
We may formulate it thus: Act so that in your own judgement and
in the judgement of others you may merit eternity. (*The Tragic
Sense of Life*, p. 263)

My own will responds to, gives assent to Unamuno. I pray at
the altars of my forefathers, relish their village tales, and their
festivals. Vaihinger might well respond that Cooley's concept
of "human nature" and Unamuno's of human "charity" are
but blessed fictions and irrational, yet nonetheless necessary,
constructs. That which is certainly continuous in the thought
of most of the people, whether theist or not, whom I have
quoted in this chapter is this simple recognition of the need for
continuity, fictive or not.

I hesitated earlier in the chapter when quoting Malinowski,
Eliade, and Unamuno to thrust the religious dimension of the
human will into the discussion until it was necessary. We can
perhaps go no further. The impulses of art, of philosophy, in
particular of ethics, sociology, and even, Vaihinger would
say, science, all flow into the metaphysical or religious dimension from which they in fact gain their hypotheses, structures
and forms. What the line of thought I have been tracing has
postulated is the absolute, the desperate, need for continuity
in the modern soul. The eighteenth century could say, "If
God did not exist, it would be necessary to invent Him." It
could be formulated then in the subjunctive mode as a process
rather unnecessary for that less chaotic time. We have come to
our full desperation in the twentieth century, and the formulations of Nietzsche, Vaihinger, Unamuno and the others have
come to this: "If God does not exist, it is necessary for us to
invent Him." The subjunctive mode has been replaced by the
imperative mode (though the "if" remains, and—so assert
Malinowski and Eliade—always will). Continuity is the bedrock need of the human spirit, and must be so so long as man
endures. One might feel that one is living quite well without
God, within the context of a cherished idealism concerning a

social or economic, philosophic or aesthetic dream, but the dream can only be based on an assumption of a cosmic assent to the dream. Such is the nature of idealisms. The critic can study the continuities, the inner harmonies of the dream, but the honest metacritic of some humility will be aware that there is no foundation for *any* given human idealism unless it be built on the firmament of the truth of a higher dream.

Notes

1. Without an appeal to the "Will of God," one falls back in ethical discussion to the "will of man," to illusions of absolutism, to the "logic of situations," to "play" principles, i.e., the "totally engrossing hold" of a given aesthetic or social context. In such a diminished condition, one can abstractly examine the condition, as does for example G. E. Moore in his *Ethics* (London, 1912), especially in his last chapter on "Intrinsic Value," or one can dramatize the ethical distinctions one can make within a social context, as does for example Henry Fielding in *Tom Jones*. That I prefer reading Fielding to Moore is perhaps obvious.

2. My own attempt at dramatizing this social and ethical context is a small illustrated arts-volume, *East Utica* (1971), published by the Munson-Williams-Proctor Institute of Utica, New York.

3. For a similar point of view, beautifully expressed, see Michael Novak, "The Family Out of Favor," *Harpers Magazine*, April 1976.

8
The Categorical Mind

> I shall therefore be extreamly careful and exact in recounting such material Passages of this Nature, as I have been able to collect. . . .Nor do I at all question, but they will furnish Plenty of noble Matter for such, whose converting Imaginations dispose them to reduce all Things into *Types;* who can make *Shadows*, no thanks to the Sun; and then mold them into Substances, no thanks to Philosophy; whose peculiar Talent lies in fixing Tropes and Allegories to the *Letter*, and refining what is Literal into Figure and Mystery.
>
> Swift, *A Tale of a Tub*, sec. 11.

I. Introductory: On Categorical Abstractions

The attempt in the previous chapter was to argue for the application to the analysis of social contexts of what have seemed to me the valid principles of literary criticism. Those principles would define criticism as the accurate response to, and precise articulation of, the unique tone and continuity of tone of a unique context, literary or societal. In the last half of my *The Rape of Cinderella*, I attempted, after a critical analysis of Hart Crane's *The Bridge*, to analyze all the previous analyses, in the hope of demonstrating that when the act of criticism of the unique text is not well done, generalities about the text are bound to be imprecise. Most of the analyses of *The Bridge* prove in fact to be the impositioning of prejudgments and precut patterns on the poem. Imposition of patterns drawn from preformed abstractions and generalizations in any area of intellectual life is the typical symptom of the categorical mind. The description of the categorical mind has already found its quintessential expression in Swift, in the involuted, subtle, and wonderful satire of *A Tale of a Tub*, *The Battle of the Books*, and *Gulliver's Travels*, and all I propose to do in this chapter is to touch on a few of its major manifestations as they have impinged on my consciousness in my own primarily literary studies.

In the previous chapter I spoke of the positive effects of family, cultural heritage, and neighborhood in the unique ethnic milieu in which I grew up in America. I alluded too to "shocks" suffered in the years at college and university as one young man came to realize just how fragile and rare is the gift of a rich context of early and local loves. My responses to these shocks constitute, I have no doubt, a large portion of my intellectual life since. So many of those intellectual experiences were in fact and in retrospect confrontations with categorical opinions that a brief outline of them is relevant here.

The basic experience was to find as I met some of my classmates in the early weeks at Kenyon College that many of them did not seem to have a similar emotional center of loves concerning family and neighborhood, that for many, separation from these at college was a relief. My homesickness made many of them uncomfortable and the more aggressive of these made it clear that they saw my melancholy as an "Oedipal" weakness to be overcome.

The general unsureness of young people about themselves—I can now see—manifested itself then in the customary arrogancies (especially, it seemed to me, among those with thin roots in a local context), and the barrage of absolutist opinions concerning all things social, ethical, political, created the conditions for the weeds of smug group-think (which I have found so often since in academic gardens). I remember especially in those early dormitory arguments (I soon stopped arguing) my bewilderment concerning the concept of "rights," which seemed crucial to each debate: that is, the individual's "right" to anything at all, even to "Life, Liberty and the Pursuit of Happiness," which so many of my classmates seemed to consider fundamental law in the universe. It was most probably my immigrant upbringing that made me question whether an individual has any "right" to expect anything at all from life, whether he must assume that any good one gets from life is a lucky break. To the close, struggling immigrant family the world is a place where nothing outside the house is taken for granted, and where yet the love and obligations within the house give meaning to life. The *rights* to freedom and pursuit of happiness, I used to argue to my classmates, could only have been understood by Jefferson as useful fictions, unless sanctioned by a Higher Power; "endowed by their Creator" was also in his formulation.[1]

As with "rights" and "freedom," I found as my college years passed that I had a distrust for abstract language and categorical absolutes in general. Concepts of man, sex, society, and so forth, came to seem like rhetorical blunderbusses; I came to be gun-shy of abstractions, even of capitalized nouns; and I came to see the cocksureness of my freshman colleagues everywhere, in the behavior of so many others older but hardly wiser, in so much of the media, and in such a large proportion of the "criticism" I was reading, whether on "Literature" or on "Man" or on "Society." The disciples and descendants of, say, to use the cliché, Darwin, Marx, and Freud, seemed in a conspiracy to destroy my cherished set of local loves and values while offering as a recompense only capitalized abstractions, the Higher Man, the Higher State or Whatever.

I was not in fact concentrating in humanistic studies as an undergraduate, but in chemistry. And strangely, I thought then, I was finding the same sort of bewildering, empty abstractions at the heart of the physical explanations of the material universe. I had a vague sense of a rightness—though it bothered me—in Swift's satire of the "giant" scientists who examine Gulliver:

> After much Debate, they concluded unanimously that I was only *Relplum Scalcath*, which is interpreted literally *Lusus Naturae*, a Determination exactly agreeable to the Modern Philosophy of

Europe: whose Professors, disdaining the old *Evasion of occult Causes*, whereby the Followers of *Aristotle* endeavour in vain to disguise their Ignorance, have invented this wonderful Solution of all Difficulties, to the unspeakable Advancement of human Knowledge.

Gulliver's Travels, Bk. II, chap. 3

Pigeonholing, that is, pretending to be an explanation; in this case a categorization productive of nothing. Not so usually in science, I was quick to tell myself then, where a given hypothesis might well be productive of a good deal of utility or beauty. I have remained in awe of what science can do and has done for men's lives. But the awareness of the limits of science in satisfying the passional needs of many men, including of course myself, for personal loves and for a sense of permanence caused me to decide a good many years ago to resist all "scientific" formulations about life that do not leave enough room for passional needs, for one's local context of personal loves, for art and religion generally, and for tolerance of the diversity of specific customs, cultures, and beliefs.

Over the two decades since my undergraduate days, I have found much scaffolding and buttressing for the positions I had taken (and still take). Karl Popper, for instance:

In so far as scientific statements refer to the world of experience, they must be refutable; and, in so far as they are irrefutable, they do not refer to the world of experience. . . . The scientific view of the definition "A puppy is a young dog" would be that it is an answer to the question *"What shall we call* a young dog?" rather than an answer to the question *"What is* a puppy?" (Questions like *"What is* life?" or *"What is* gravity?" do not play any role in science.)

The Open Society and Its Enemies vol. 2, pp. 12, 14

Hans Vaihinger, for another:

It is the ambition of science, we saw, to make of the world of ideas an ever more useful instrument for dealing with things and for action. The world of ideas which results from this ambition, and which we generally call "truth" is consequently only the most expedient error, i.e., that system of ideas which enables us to act and to deal with things most rapidly, neatly and safely, and with the minimum of irrational elements. . . . (*The Philosophy of "As If,"* p. 108)

These attitudes towards knowledge stand in the greatest possible contrast to those of the prophets of history and social change, visionaries of cosmic consciousness and universal archetypes, absolutists and dogmatists about the human condition, or devotees to a given idea or system. Arrogance is the attitude that pervades the categorical mind, the certainty that one has the archetypal key to one universal truth or another. It is to some manifestations of this sort of thinking that I want now to turn.

II. Freudianism and Archetypalism

i. Freud: Sexuality as Reductive Category

The Freudian dialectic embodies a pretense of absolute knowledge of our psychic origins, of the evolution of the individual psyche from childhood to adulthood, and also of the universal evolution of the human psyche from primal to civilized man. Freud provided during different times in his career various dualistic categories of discourse which he consistently asserted led back to a unitary archetypal key for the explanation of universal human behavior. The process is reductive, and impelled by the simple desire for the abstraction of universals out of experience.

Karl Popper's view of Freudianism, from his perspective as a philosopher of scientific logic, is that it must finally be termed a "pseudo-science":

Those "clinical observations" which analysts naively believe confirm their theory cannot do this any more than the daily confirmations which astrologers find in their practice. And as for Freud's epic of the Ego, the Super-ego, and the Id, no substantially stronger claim to scientific status can be made for it than for Homer's collected stories from Olympus. These theories describe some facts, but in the manner of myths. They contain most interesting psychological suggestions, but not in a testable form. (*Conjectures and Refutations*, pp. 37–38)

The position is, surprisingly, typical of a wide spectrum of scientists and social scientists.[2] Popper however spends little effort in demonstrating his position. The book that has come in a short time to occupy a preeminent position as a critical evaluation of Freudianism is Henri Ellenberger's *The Discovery of the Unconscious* (1970). Ellenberger has great respect for much in Freud; it becomes clear, however, as one reads Ellenberger's book why it is that one, especially perhaps the literary person, is surprised to find, when he looks, so many negative assessments of Freudianism from impressive quarters. The outsider to the controversies, the student who has read much about Freudianism but little Freud, is laboring with a legend partially the creation of Freud and his tightly controlled disciples, partially the creation of popular culture:

A rapid glance at the Freudian legend reveals two main features. The first is the theme of the solitary hero struggling against a host of enemies, suffering "the slings and arrows of outrageous fortune" but triumphing in the end. The legend considerably exaggerates the extent and role of antiSemitism, and the hostility of the academic world, and of alleged Victorian prejudices. The second feature of the Freudian legend is the blotting out of the greatest part of the scientific and cultural context in which psychoanalysis developed, hence the theme of the absolute originality of the achievements, in which the hero is credited with the achievements of his predecessors, associates, disciples, rivals, and contemporaries. (P. 547)

Ellenberger painstakingly refutes the legend and restores the scientific and cultural context. Even more importantly, he demonstrates by close and chronological analysis of Freud's work the many shifts in theoretic ground underlying the superficially monolithic theory of psychoanalysis, as Freud's metapsychological speculations caused him to ceaselessly modify the dualistic terms of his dialectic. I want to attempt now to demonstrate the Freudian reductive methodology in operation, aided in places by Ellenberger's analyses and conclusions.

If I now declare that wish-fulfillment is the meaning of *every* dream, so that there cannot be any dreams other than wish-dreams, I know beforehand that I shall meet with the most emphatic contradiction. . . . The anxiety-dream does really seem to preclude a generalization of the thesis deduced from the examples given in the last chapter, that dreams are wish-fulfillments, and even to condemn it as an absurdity.

Nevertheless, it is not difficult to parry these apparently invincible objections. It is merely necessary to observe that our doctrine is not based upon the estimates of the obvious dream-content, but relates to the thought-content, which, in the course of interpretation, is found to lie behind the dream. Let us compare and contrast the *manifest* and the *latent dream-content*. It is true that there are dreams the manifest content of which is of the most painful nature. But has anyone ever tried to interpret these dreams—to discover their latent thought-content? If not, the two objections to our doctrine are no longer valid; for there is always the possibility that even our painful and terrifying dreams may, upon interpretation, prove to be wish-fulfillments. . . . If my dream, as compared with its latent content, is disguised at this point, and actually misrepresents things by producing their opposites, then the manifest affection in the dream serves the purpose of the misrepresentation; in other words, the distortion is here shown to be intentional—it is a means of *disguise*. . . . This discovery may prove to be generally valid. . . .

The detailed correspondence between the phenomena of censorship and the phenomena of dream-distortion justifies us in presupposing similar conditions for both. We should then assume that in every human being there exist, as the primary cause of dream-formation, two psychic forces (tendencies or systems), one of which forms the wish expressed by the dream, while the other exercises a censorship over this dream-wish, thereby enforcing on it a distortion. . . . (*The Interpretation of Dreams*, in *The Basic Writings of Sigmund Freud*, pp. 217–18, 222–23)

The statements are a tissue of hypotheses and assumptions dependent entirely on "interpretation" and "correspondences." The assertions are really these: "all dreams are fulfillments of wishes; when they do not seem to be, it is because the dream's latent (unconscious) content is the opposite of its manifest (conscious) content; it is so because that is how I interpret all dreams." Yet the apostate Jung and the revisionist Fromm interpret Freud's case-dreams quite differently (see below, pp. 159–61), both rejecting the wish-fulfillment hypothesis. Freud's confidence moves in two paragraphs from "this discovery *may* prove to be generally valid" to "We should then assume that in *every* human being. . . ." The shift into certainty is based on "a parallel in social life" and the "correspondence" to the "political writer" who is "in fear of censorship," and the hypothesis thereby created is one conveniently (compulsively) of two opposing psychic forces, one "proletariat" and the other "bourgeoisie" (later to be called the *Id* and the *Ego*). It is not the assumption of the simple existence of unconscious psychic life in the individual that is dubious here, but the patently unproved (unprovable?) assumption that the unconscious is always and necessarily at war with the conscious, a position that can only breed, has bred, dangerous corollary assumptions, such as that an individual's unconscious motives are necessarily the opposite of his conscious motives, or to be more specific, an artist's unconscious intentions are necessarily the opposite of his conscious intentions.

Such assumptions are not to be refuted by any supposed counter evidence, such as a patient dreaming dreams which apparently run counter to the theory:

> If I group together the very frequent dreams of this sort, which seem flatly to contradict my theory, in that they embody the denial of a wish or some occurrence obviously undesired, under the head of "counter-wish-dreams," I find that they may all be referred to two principles, one of which has not yet been mentioned, though it plays a large part in waking as well as dream-life. One of the motives inspiring these dreams is the wish that I

should appear in the wrong. These dreams occur regularly in the course of treatment whenever the patient is in a state of resistance. . . . (P. 233)

It cannot be that he is wrong, because he is well on his way to the desired *summa*—a simple solution to all psychical and metaphysical problems:

> Further, since experience in dream-analysis has drawn my attention to the fact that even from dreams the interpretation of which seems at first sight complete, because the dream-sources and the wish-stimuli are easily demonstrable, important trains of thought proceed which reach back into the earliest years of childhood. I had to ask myself whether this characteristic does not even constitute an essential condition of dreaming. If it were permissible to generalize this notion, I should say that every dream is connected through its manifest content with recent experiences, while through its latent content it is connected with the most remote experiences; and I can actually show in the analysis of hysteria that these remote experiences have in a very real sense remained recent right up to the present. But I shall find it very difficult to prove this conjecture; I shall have to return to the probable role in dream-formation of the earliest experiences of our childhood in another connection (Chapter VII). (Pp. 275–76)

"If it were permissible to generalize this notion, I should say that . . ." How humble! "Notion" and "conjecture." How honest, how scientific! Not to fear; the hero will be right in the end (Chapter VII).

He will do it by the incontrovertible appeal to "incidental observation" and "legendary matter":

> It is far more probable—and this is confirmed by incidental observations of normal children—that in their amorous or hostile attitude toward their parents, psychoneurotics do no more than reveal to us, by magnification, something that occurs less markedly and intensively in the minds of the majority of children. Antiquity has furnished us with legendary matter which corroborates this belief, and the profound and universal validity of the old

legends is explicable only by an equally universal validity of the above-mentioned hypothesis of infantile psychology. (P. 307)

Not to worry about the disturbing phrase "the majority of children"; rest assured that the hypothesis will soon (next page) encompass *all* children. It transpires too that "the profound and universal validity of the old legends" is demonstrated by the interpretations of psychoanalysis at the same time that it is the legends that confirm the "equally universal validity" of the psychoanalytic hypothesis (much as in Wallace Stevens's phrase in "Esthetique du Mal," "hunger feeding on its own hungriness," or, in the vernacular of the street-poet, "one hand washing the other").

> If the *Oedipus Rex* is capable of moving a modern reader or playgoer no less powerfully than it moved the contemporary Greeks, the only possible explanation is that the effect of the Greek tragedy does not depend upon the conflict between fate and human will, but upon the peculiar nature of the material by which this conflict is revealed. There must be a voice within us which is prepared to acknowledge the compelling power of fate in the *Oedipus*. . . . And there actually is a motive in the story of King Oedipus which explains the verdict of this inner voice. His fate moves us only because it might have been our own, because the oracle laid upon us before our birth the very curse which rested upon him. It may be that we were all destined to direct our first sexual impulses toward our mothers, and our first impulses of hatred and violence toward our fathers; our dreams convince us that we were. King Oedipus, who slew his father Laius and wedded his mother Jocasta, is nothing more or less than a wish-fulfillment—the fulfillment of the wish of our childhood. But we, more fortunate than he, in so far as we have not become psychoneurotics, have since our childhood succeeded in withdrawing our sexual impulses from our mothers, and in forgetting our jealousy of our fathers. (P. 308)

Oedipus of course in the old legend did not know that he was killing his father and marrying his mother, and he did feel the gods were unjust to him. But, Freud would assert, this is all manifest content and therefore worthless; the play is universal because its latent content confirms Freud's hypothesis of infantile sexual psychology, and our unconscious knows it. This, says Freud, is the "only possible explanation" of the play's powerful effect on us; that is, Oedipus as sexual neurotic.

Thus have we the oracle laid upon us, and thus are we prepared for the final aforepromised archetypal solution of chapter 7:

> every dream may be a wish-fulfillment, but there must be other forms of abnormal wish-fulfillment as well as dreams. And in fact the theory of all psychoneurotic symptoms culminates in the one proposition *that they, too, must be conceived as wish-fulfillments of the unconscious.* Our explanation makes the dream only the first member of a series of the greatest importance for the psychiatrist, the understanding of which means the solution of the purely psychological part of the psychiatric problem. (P. 511)

But why stop here at the "purely psychological part" when there are so many other worlds to conquer?

> I want to state the conclusion that the beginnings of religion, ethics, society, and art meet in the Oedipus complex. This is in entire accord with the findings of psychoanalysis, namely, that the nucleus of all neuroses as far as our present knowledge of them goes is the Oedipux complex. It comes as a great surprise to me that these problems of racial psychology can also be solved through a single concrete instance, such as in the relation to the father (*Totem and Taboo*, in *Basic Writings*, p. 927)

Can it really, one cannot help asking, have come as a great surprise to Freud that a "single concrete instance" can solve all problems, when the monist compulsion to find such a key of keys is everywhere evident in all that he writes?[3]

Such are the humble beginnings of the grand Freudian edifice: (1) the interpretation of dreams (which he calls the "via regia to the knowledge of the unconscious element in our psychic life," p. 540), about which there is little agreement and less scientific proof; and (2) the assumption of the universality of the Oedipus complex, which, is so far as it is provable, was very quickly proven to be false:

> In the Trobriands there is no friction between father and son, and all the infantile craving of the child for its mother is allowed gradually to spend itself in a natural, spontaneous manner. . . . it appears necessary to draw in more systematically the correlation between biological and social influences; not to assume the universal existence of the Oedipus complex, but in studying every type of civilization, to establish the special complex which pertains to it. (Bronislaw Malinowski, in *Theories of Society*, ed. T. Parsons et al., vol. 1, pp. 277–78 [from *Sex & Repression in Savage Society*, 1927])

> One conclusion stands out above all others: emotional development, as couched in terms of successive object choices, is far more variable than Freud supposed. This is not to say that none of the classical elements appears. They do; but with too many exceptions to be accepted as typical. . . . Freud was able to abstract one of the not too uncommon developmental patterns. But other sequences have been observed, too, and lead inescapably to the conclusion that Freud vastly underrated the importance of the child's immediate social milieu as a source for these kinds of learning, and overrated the uniformity of family patterns. (Robert R. Sears, *Survey of Objective Studies of Psychoanalytic Concepts*, pp. 57, 137)

The later essays of Freud modify the theoretical system of *The Interpretation of Dreams*, though not its fundamental reductive position, which is that "the theory of the psychoneuroses asserts with absolute certainty that it can only be sexual wish-impulses from the infantile life, which . . . supply the motive-power for all psychoneurotic symptom-formation" (p. 538). The Oedipus complex comes to be subdivided into the "simple" and the "more complete" which is

> twofold, positive and negative, and is due to the bisexuality originally present in children. . . . It is this complicating element introduced by bisexuality that makes it so difficult to obtain a

clear view of the facts in connection with the earliest object-choices and identifications, and still more difficult to describe them intelligibly. It may even be that the ambivalence displayed in the relations to the parents should be attributed entirely to bisexuality and that it is not, as I have represented above, developed out of identification in consequence of rivalry.

In my opinion it is advisable in general, and quite especially where neurotics are concerned, to assume the existence of the complete Oedipus complex. ("The Ego and the Id," in *The Complete Psychological Works of Sigmund Freud*, vol. 19, p. 33.)

What is clear to this reader is Freud's barely repressed wish to drop the "simple" Oedipus complex from his equations of infantile sexuality and adult psychoneuroses:

. . .fresh problems arise, from which one is tempted to draw cautiously back. But there is no help for it, the attempt must be made—in spite of a fear that it will lay bare the inadequacy of our whole effort. The question is: which was it, the ego of primitive man or his id, that acquired religion and morality in those early days out of the father-complex? If it was his ego, why do we not speak simply of these things being inherited by the ego? If it was the id, how does that agree with the character of the id? Or are we wrong in carrying the differentiation between ego, superego, and id back into such early times? Or should we not honestly confess that our whole conception of the processes in the ego is of no help in understanding phylogenesis and cannot be applied to it? (Pp. 37–38)

The hero will fight these fears that his terms are useless fictions and will make temporary "conquests" or adjustments, spinning threads from out of the Oedipus complex, the "bisexuality" theory, the castration complex in males and the penis envy in females. The fears and the adjustments, such as they are, continue till the end in Freud's work:

When we speak of an 'archaic heritage' we are usually thinking only of the id and we seem to assume that at the beginning of the individual's life no ego is as yet in existence. But we shall not overlook the fact that id and ego are originally one; nor does it imply any mystical overvaluation of heredity if we think it credible that, even before the ego has come into existence, the lines of development, trends and reactions which it will later exhibit are already laid down for it. . . .

With the recognition that the properties of the ego which we meet with in the form of resistances can equally well be determined by heredity as acquired in defensive struggles, the topographical distinction between what is ego and what is id loses much of its value for our investigation. . . .

Both in therapeutic and in character-analyses we notice that two themes come into especial prominence and give the analyst an unusual amount of trouble. . . .

The two corresponding themes are in the female, an *envy for the penis*—a positive striving to possess a male genital—and, in the male, a struggle against his passive or feminine attitude to another male. . . .

No transference can arise from the female's wish for a penis, but it is the source of outbreaks of severe depression in her, owing to an internal conviction that the analysis will be of no use and that nothing can be done to help her. And we can only agree that she is right, when we learn that her strongest motive in coming for treatment was the hope that, after all, she might still obtain a male organ, the lack of which was so painful to her. . . .

We often have the impression that with the wish for a penis and the masculine protest we have penetrated through all the psychological strata and have reached bedrock, and that thus our activities are at an end. ("Analysis Terminable and Interminable," *The Complete Psychological Works of Sigmund Freud* vol. 23, pp. 240, 241, 250, 252.)

Some bedrock! Some activity! This final essay, with its throwing up of the hands concerning various obsessions of his life, is but the culmination of a profound pessimism that seems to dominate Freud after World War I. It is this pessimism which—as Ellenberger points out—may in part account (along with Freud's fears about "the inadequacy of our whole effort") for the incessant reworking of the abstract dualistic categories upon which Freud bases his system,[+] from, among others, ego-id to pleasure-unpleasure to love-death, the final, all-embracing pair:

> Only by the concurrent or mutually opposing action of the two primal instincts—Eros and the death-instinct—, never by one or the other alone, can we explain the rich multiplicity of the phenomena of life. (P. 243)

This is a modern sexualized brand of manichean dualism, which explains nothing as it pretends to explain everything:

> I am well aware that the dualistic theory according to which an instinct of death or of destruction or aggression claims equal rights as a partner with Eros as manifested in the libido, has found little sympathy, and has not really been accepted even among psychoanalysts. (P. 244)

The statement and the essay are at least clear, as Freud should have been clear in all of his writing, about the speculative, conjectural nature of his theories and of his categories of discourse:

> Without metapsychological speculation and theorizing—I had almost said 'phantasying'—we shall not get another step forward. Unfortunately, here as elsewhere, what our Witch reveals is neither very clear nor very detailed. . . .
> It is impossible to define health except in metapsychological terms: i.e. by reference to the dynamic relations between the agencies of the mental apparatus which have been recognized—or (if that is preferred) inferred or conjectured—by us. . . .
> We may say that analysis, in claiming to cure neuroses by ensuring control over instinct, is always right in theory but not always right in practice. (Pp. 225, 226, 229)

And the essay is honest about the irresolution that elsewhere one finds underlying so much of the deceptive Freudian rhetoric of certainty, absolutes, and universals. Freud's fondness for "every," "all," and "only" is typical of the categorical mind. It is a rhetoric which characteristically shifts quickly from speculation to hypothesis to dogma. Vaihinger finds this process so usual in psychology and history that he formulates a "Law of Ideational Shifts":

> It is to the effect that a number of ideas pass through various stages of development, namely those of fiction, hypothesis and dogma; and conversely dogma, hypothesis and fiction. (*The Philosophy of "As If," p. 124*)

The Oedipus complex, castration complex, the theories of infantile sexuality as the basis of all psychoneuroses, those of wish-fulfillment, of the nature of ego-id, of the love-death instinct, and so forth are fictions that can be called hypotheses only insofar as they are (in Popper's terms) testable and refutable—which has proven to be not very far. The theoretical system of psychoanalysis seems to be losing ground rapidly as dogma.[5] Its future career will thus most likely depend, from Vaihinger's perspective, on whether its fictions come to be seen as indispensable, or at the very least useful, to social organization, as, say, the ideas of freedom, rights, or human dignity have been seen. It does seem to this observer that they will prove to be.

The universality of the Oedipus complex specifically, is a dogma that represses the critical spirit, a dogma which if accepted would discourage the close investigation of a given social context and its uniqueness within its own continuities, and thus result in inaccurate, imprecise social criticism. And it seems to me that Freudianism in general has helped to create a climate in America of fear and embarrassment over familial love except for the love of husband and wife, and even that has come too often to be seen in terms of mutual sexual egoism. Love of children for parents, parents for children, has come to be seen in the Oedipal situation as sublimation of incestuous, aggressive, and infantile drives. What has happened is that the reductionism inherent in the dialectic methodology of the Freudian theory has helped foster a reductionism in the cultural idea of love, and a cultural idea (*folkway* in Sumner's language, *fiction* in Vaihinger's), whether reductive or expansive, can have enormous force in a given society. A false theoretical idea sufficiently propagandized can cause the effect to come into being which the idea had postulated as a prior cause. The suspicion of motive in all things, in personal relations and sentiments, in social, political, and religious idealism, or in artistic intention, has contributed—who knows to what degree—to a popular culture of superficiality and barrenness concerning sexual, family, social, and religious matters.

Human needs for value, meaning, warmth seem so obviously to run deeper than the equally obvious sexual needs which dominate our modern cultural definitions of love. It may be argued that our ideas of love and God are in fact the supreme, the most indispensable "fictions" or hypotheses for us, the most profound "illusions"—if they be illusions—which give us the chance for the deepest-rooted values. And it may be argued too that if in fact there is no scientific "truth" that can equate to our needs, there is, in such a human predicament, no obligation to settle for the most dubious, least useful, of Freudian fictions, of the Id, or Oedipus, or worse.[6]

I can agree more with sociological formulations such as, say, W. I. Thomas's:

> The importance of recognition and status for the individual and for society is very great. The individual not only wants them but he needs them for the development of his personality. The lack of them and the fear of never obtaining them are probably the main source of those psychopathic disturbances which the Freudians treat as sexual in origin. "The Four Wishes and the Definition of the Situation," in *Theories of Society*, vol. 2, p. 742.

But I can agree most with the individual analyst, be he novelist or critic or social scientist (like Thomas), who pores over the unique social or aesthetic context, the unique individuals within it, and respects the integrity of the persons and the context for as long as he can—at least till that time that he feels he can make the minimum necessary generalizations with the maximum accuracy and precision possible.

ii. Freudian Literary Criticism: Latent Error, Manifest Nonsense

It is not to be expected that much real criticism will come from the categorical mind, Freudian or otherwise oriented, since respect for the context takes second place to the mono-mania, sexual or other. It has been argued that whatever the merits of Freud's findings, his emphasis on the unconscious and on sexuality opened these areas for twentieth-century art-ists. I think the converse can be argued, has been argued by Ellenberger and others: that scholars and artists of the nineteenth century opened these areas for Freud. I would argue further that little of major twentieth-century art has adopted Freudian dogmatics (though much of its "atmospher-ics"), and that Freudian dogmatics as applied to the arts has produced a Freudian "criticism" of a very low order.

What Freudian criticism is consistently doing with literary texts and with the arts in general is ignoring the body of attitudes expressed in a given work of art as but "manifest," hence irrelevant, content, while offering to the uninitiated, the true "latent" content. Of this content everybody, includ-ing the author, has been unaware, and it has to do of course and interminably with the sexual writhings of the "libido." Remarks like those of Alan Friedman (see above, p. 80–81) on passages in *The Rainbow* as "transcriptions of the Underself" which remain "unavailable to the consciousness" are untypical only in that Friedman is sensitive to the stylistic discontinuity of the passages within the "manifest" content. Yet the message is the same; the *adepti* know the truth, and we are to take it on faith that Lawrence also has it, no matter that it is for us unknowable, inarticulable, and in fact, so far as we can see, self-contradictory.

My introduction to Freudian criticism in my undergraduate years was particularly memorable. I had been profoundly moved by Kafka's *Trial* and fell then unfortunately into Charles Neider's *The Frozen Sea* (N.Y., 1948):

> The discovery of a key to Kafka's novels was made only gradually . . . .
>
> Joseph K.'s arrest is a symbolic one. It is not caused by a civil authority. He is not incarcerated. It is a psychic arrestation, a fixation classical in neurosis. He is arrested on the anal level of sexual development. And he is the victim of a castration complex . . . .
>
> Scoptophilia is an element of the anal stage. Joseph K. is a chronic voyeur . . . .
>
> The wardens, like K.'s assistants in *The Castle*, symbolize Joseph K's testicles and his deficient sexuality . . . .
>
> Kafka's novels comprise a fictional equivalent of the infancy period in the human's sexual development, as outlined by psychoanalysis. The three sub-stages of this period, the oral, the anal, and the early genital, are represented by *Amerika*, *The Trial* and *The Castle* respectively . . . . K. is the only one of the three protagonists who is genital—and he is only partially genital, because of his Oedipus fixation. (Pp. vii, 153, 167, 172, 183)

All this dismaying reductionism despite the fact that Neider does not consider himself a devotee of the psychoanalytic movement—

> I should like to say that the presence of psychoanalytic material in my book I consider an accident—Kafka's responsibility, for I am convinced that he deliberately placed it in the novels . . . . (P. vii)

—and despite the fact that he considers Kafka a great novelist. And I was of course soon exposed to Dr. Ernest Jones's Hamlet:

> Hamlet is suffering from an internal conflict the essential nature of which is inaccessible to his introspection . . . . the more intense and the more obscure is a given case of deep mental conflict the more certainly will it be found on adequate analysis to center about a sexual problem. On the surface, of course, this does not appear so, for, by means of various psychological defen-

sive mechanisms, the depression, doubt, despair, and other manifestations of the conflict are transferred on to more tolerable and
permissible topics, such as anxiety about worldly success or failure, about immortality and the salvation of the soul, philosophical
considerations about the value of life, the future of the world, and
so on.

Bearing these considerations in mind, let us return to Hamlet
. . . . Now comes the father's death and the mother's second
marriage. The association of the idea of sexuality with his mother,
buried since infancy, can no longer be concealed from his consciousness . . . . Without his being in the least aware of it these
ancient desires are ringing in his mind, are once more struggling
to find conscious expression, and need such an expenditure of
energy again to "repress" them that he is reduced to the deplor-
able mental state he himself so vividly depicts. (*Hamlet and
Oedipus*, pp. 52, 59, 82 [first published in 1910])

That is, Hamlet hasn't the faintest idea as to what is wrong
with him; the content of his soliloquies is quite irrelevant to
his situation, whether Shakespeare knows it or not. Jones will
not, any more than his mentor Freud, allow a tragedy to be
about tragic (permissible) topics, but only about sexual (im-
permissible) ones.

To the psychoanalytic critic, Hart Crane's symbol of the
Bridge will predictably mean a phallus (or the lack of one):

Whether the dreamer be a woman who has not yet accepted her
femininity, or a man with a deep castration anxiety, the inability
to cross the bridge may in either case represent the incapacity for
heterosexual intercourse . . . . Crane was racked by this "love of
things irreconcilable": the incestuous love of the mother, and the
sterile love of man for man. It is . . . . a striking example of a work
of a creative imagination which thwarts the intentions of its author. (Paul Friedman, "*The Bridge:* A Study in Symbolism," pp.
56, 74.)

Why striking, one wonders, when *all* works of the creative
imagination end up in psychoanalytic interpretation as examples of the author's sexual anxieties and Oedipal repressions,
and *all* unbeknownst to the author? Here, the homosexual

poet's poetry must be about his homosexuality beneath all that manifest intentional content. But the author's homosexuality is perhaps the least interesting subject—if it is there at all—of all those that are there in *The Bridge*.[8] And the least of the sins of the Freudian critic—leaving aside the wreck he usually makes, if he does not ignore it, of the unique and subtle "manifest" context—is the tedious, repetitive reduction of all aesthetic discussion to off-the-cuff analysis of the sexual problems of the artist.

Freud often expressed his profound admiration for artists and their achievements, even going so far as to say that psychoanalysis could not explain genius.[9] But whenever Freud gets down to business he seems to have little trouble forcing the greatest of art and the least of jokes into the preordained mold. The reductionism worked on *Oedipus Rex* (see above, p. 147) would no doubt have struck Sophocles much as the mortal blow of Clytemnestra struck Agamemnon. The mysteries of the expressions of Leonardo da Vinci's Mona Lisa and St. Anne lie for Freud in da Vinci's childhood, in his— you guessed it—Oedipus complex (see Freud's *A Childhood Memory of Leonardo da Vinci*, and Ellenberger, *The Discovery of the Unconscious*, pp. 520–21). Meyer Shapiro's scholarly examination of Freud's da Vinci ("Leonardo and Freud," published in the *Journal of the History of Ideas*) demonstrates Freud's imprecision concerning the facts of da Vinci's childhood and also the traditional nature of many of the symbols and motifs in da Vinci which Freud postulates as keys to da Vinci's unconscious and hence to his personal analysis.[10]

A final example. When I came to a close study of the criticism of Joyce's *Ulysses* for my *The Rape of Cinderella*, I found as generally accepted opinion the ideas that (1) Molly Bloom was promiscuous, to be seen as either a talking Id or a mythic Earth Mother, and that (2) the "Nighttown" episode in Bella Cohen's brothel was an objectifying of the unconscious life of the minds of Stephen Dedalus and Leopold Bloom. Neither position is at all precise. The evidence in the text is that (1) Molly's rendezvous that day with Blazes Boylan is her first venture into adultery, and that she is a rather decent, ordinary woman who is as a consequence suffering some pain, sadness, and guilt, and that (2) the flow of absurd surrealistic vignettes in the "Nighttown" episode are demonstrably not stream-of-unconscious of either Stephen or Bloom, but conscious highly-wrought stream-of-artifice of their author, highly sophisticated parody of literary reflex. I refer the reader to my essay for the documentation of this position, which is not very novel any more. The point is that general precision concerning such a major novel is obviously dependent on precision concerning such textual details. Yet so pervasive the influence of Freudianism in the intellectual life of the first half of this century that the evidence in the text, despite many recent critical efforts, still struggles for recognition.

Imprecision concerning local texture and context is a small matter to those who, like Freud, are imposing a system from above. It is the reader who must beware whenever any "critic," Freudian or otherwise, sets as his job of work the application of his universal dialectic onto a large number of literary works, for it will not be the work only that is thereby reduced, but the reader as well.

iii. On Jungian Archetypes, and Archetypal vs. "Deconstructive" Criticism

In the absence of any real evidence for Freud's theoretical interpretation of dreams as wish fulfillment of the libido, there quickly emerged psychological counter theories, notably those of Carl Jung. Jung rejects the ideas of dreams being exclusively wish-fulfilling or exclusively sexual, rejects the necessary dualism of manifest and latent content and the censorship principle, rejects the omnipresence of the Oedipal situation in life or dreams, rejects the Freudian description of the Id in particular and of the unconscious life in general (see Ellenberger, *The Discovery of the Unconscious*, pp. 705–34). Jung sees the unconscious as the source not simply of sexual images but more fundamentally of archetypal images. Archetypal images, Jung asserts, are inherent in the human psyche; the evidence is in their recurrence in the dreams of neurotics, of normal people, and of geniuses, in primitive and sophisticated peoples, in primitive myth, folk tales, and in the highest religious and artistic expression. Their recurrence may imply a transcendent reality, a "World Soul," from which they flow, or simply that there is a universal human Psyche or Being which is manifested in these recurrent productions of our unconscious. If transcendental, one can speak of the "Cosmic Consciousness"; if not, one can speak of the "Collective Unconscious."

The Freudian sexual fixation is gone in Jung; the spectrum for symbol and dream interpretation is vastly widened. As Ellenberger puts it, "to a Freudian analyst the snake is just a phallic symbol; to a Jungian it might be this, but it also can have ten other meanings" (p. 734). Ellenberger notes too that "one basic feature of Jung's dream interpretation is his emphasis of dream series: a given dream can only be understood in the context of those that precede or follow it and sometimes of the entire set" (p. 716). This is all, and thus far, to the good, for literary criticism at any rate.[11]

But it must be also noted that there is far from agreement within non-Freudian psychoanalytic schools about the archetypes and their recurring patterns in myth and dream:

> The study of myths and dreams is still in its infancy. It suffers from various limitations. One is a certain dogmatism and rigidity that has resulted from the claims of various psychoanalytic schools, each insisting that it has the only true understanding of symbolic language. . .
>   The difference between Jung's interpretation and my own can be summed up in this statement. There is agreement that we often are wiser and more decent in our sleep than in our waking life. Jung explains this phenomenon with the assumption of a source of revelation transcending us, while I believe that what we think in our sleep is *our* thinking. (Erich Fromm, *The Forgotten Language*, pp. 9, 97)

Which is honest about the tentativeness of all psychoanalytic theories of dream interpretation or understandings of symbolic language. Yet Fromm is curiously not at all tentative about his assumptions of the *existence* of a universal symbolic language and of a collective archetypal unconscious which speaks that language:

> Symbolic language is . . . the one universal language the human race has ever developed, the same for all cultures and throughout history. It is a language with its own grammar and syntax, as it were, a language one must understand if one is to understand the meaning of myths, fairy tales and dreams. (P. 7)

If one believes in the existence of the collective unconscious (as do Fromm and Jung) or the cosmic consciousness (as does Jung), or the universal symbolic language (as do many recent mythologists, mythographers, and "structuralists"), one needs to realize, to use Popper's terms, that he is in the realm of unverified, probably unverifiable experience, and that he will not therefore easily convince the skeptic through simple assertion of their existence. Malinowski's findings on the supposed "universality" of the Oedipus complex should give pause to those "sure" about the universality of symbolic language.

In the area of literary criticism, interpretation of literary texts by means of one's knowledge of archetypal symbols and patterns has become a favorite methodology, especially since the appearance in 1957 of Northrop Frye's *Anatomy of Criticism*. Frye discounts however any dependence in his work on "Jung and his school, where the communicability of archetypes is accounted for by a theory of a collective unconscious—an unnecessary hypothesis in literary criticism, so far as I can judge" (pp. 111–12). Frye is interested in the recurrence of communicable archetypes as a "social fact" if not psychological fact, and seems simply to want to work with the effects—the symbolic language of archetypes—without any hypothesizing concerning the "cause":

> Archetype: that is, a typical or recurring image. I mean by an archetype a symbol which connects one poem with another and thereby helps to unify and integrate our literary experience. And as the archetype is the communicable symbol, archetypal criti-

cism is primarily concerned with literature as a social fact and as a mode of communication. (P. 99)

In any case, the impetus for my *The Rape of Cinderella* was Frye's book, and, for all the brilliance in its classifications of literature into types and categories, I saw then and see now such a methodology—the "connecting" of "one poem with another" by means of their shared symbols or narrative patterns—as a resting in a half-way house at some distance from the real work of criticism, which I see as the attempt at precise specification.[12] But it is a methodology which has captivated many recent researchers in literature and sociology, Frye and Claude Lévi-Strauss being only the most famous and most distinguished. The literary criticism which has flowed from this methodology, while of a far higher level than that which has flowed from psychoanalysis, still results, however, in categorizations tending toward the obliteration of the uniqueness of a given text.

I remember reading in *Sources and Analogues of Chaucer's "Canterbury Tales"* and elsewhere of the multitude of examples from various countries of the archetypal narrative pattern wherein three rioters come to a bad end by two plotting against one and the one plotting against the two, as happens in Chaucer's "Pardoner's Tale." One then moved on to the re-searching of the analogues of the recurrent motif of the wandering old man who wishes to, but cannot, die. My conclusion then: nothing in the analogues can account for the genius of the "Pardoner's Tale," especially in the brilliant context of its "Prologue" and "Epilogue." The process repeated over the years results in the wider conclusion: symbol, myth, and folk tale stay at the level of folk art till the sophisticated individual aesthetic consciousness makes them into sophisticated art; the works of Homer, Dante, Chaucer, Shakespeare, are not the sum total of the archetypal images, myths, or narrative patterns which they intuitively or consciously use.[13]

One seeks in vain in Frye's book for articulations of the precise textures and tone of a unique artistic context, for that which makes a work of genius out of a collage of typical and archetypal materials. What one finds is the connecting of "one poem with another," which can only result in a reduction worked on both; as William Wimsatt asserts:

> In his moments of most nearly pure archetypal abstraction, Frye's types are in a sense true patterns. But in that sense they are also truistic, simplistic, and uninteresting. More or less universally valid patterns of imagery and shapes of stories can of course be discerned in the canon of the world's literature. Fictional stories, it is true, are all about what we wish to have or to be and what we wish not to have or not to be, what we like and what we don't like. Love and marriage and banquets and dances and springtime and wheat and fruit and wine are good. Hate and strife and downfall and death, disease, blight, and poison, are bad. A lamb is a good animal, a wolf or a tiger is a bad one, and frightening, especially in a pastoral society or tradition. "Any symbolism founded on food," says Frye, "is universal." We can live in a city or a garden, not in a stony or weedy wilderness. If we rummage out all the ideas of the desirable and undesirable we can think of, they fall inevitably under the heads of the supernatural, the human, the animal, vegetable, and mineral. . . .
>
> Similarly, to describe Hamlet's stage-tradition jump into Ophelia's grave as if it were an instance of the classic descent into the underworld is a cliché application of the archetype, ingenious perhaps, but still a cliché, a mythopoeist's cliché. ("Northrop Frye: Criticism as Myth," in *The Day of the Leopards*, pp. 86–87)

Wimsatt (along with M. H. Abrams) is the most perceptive of modern critics concerning the dangers of categorical thinking in general, "this ruthless, categorizing, assimilative, subsuming drive" within theories which "conceive men, whether common or elite, in large multiples, thinking and responding in classes."[14]

In the decade after World War II, literary criticism in America was dominated by the voices of the so-called "New Criticism": Wimsatt, Cleanth Brooks, and René Wellek at Yale, John Crowe Ransom at Kenyon, R. P. Blackmur at Princeton, and others. Their shared concern was for the integrity of the art work—its authority and uniqueness. They saw the business of criticism as the close analysis of the tone and texture of a given text; hence their label as contextualists. (Their influence on my writing is perhaps obvious.) Various brands of archetypal criticism held center stage during the sixties. The seventies have been dominated by a "deconstructive" criticism which at first might seem the antipode to both contextualism and archetypalism. For, ontologically, the philosopher of deconstruction, Jacques Derrida, denies any meaning to the ideas of contextual cores or "centers" and of universal archetypes, both ideas implying a metaphysical centering and organizing God.[15]

But ontology is one thing, literary criticism another thing. The practitioners of "deconstructive" criticism are very much like the practitioners of archetypal criticism. With the archetypalists, all contexts are made to fit into a few textual paradigms. With the deconstructionists, since there is no such thing as a centered context, all texts flow into a vast pool of intertextuality, wherein one can swim as one will for as long as one can. The result has been a criticism as abstracted from the text as is archetypal criticism:

> . . . somewhere along the line a judgement will need to be made about the practice of the Derrideans; a judgement as to whether their essays . . . do not repeat the same point, do not allegorize texts . . . over and over in very predictable ways, and with a heavy-handedness reminiscent of mythographic and structuralist critics. (Frank Lentricchia, *After the New Criticism*, p. 182)

When literary criticism does not respect unique context, it is not functioning as criticism, but as metacriticism. The metacritical position may be ontological ("nominalistic" or "realistic") or psychological, historical or political, transcendental or nihilistic, no matter. The position is no guarantee of good criticism; if sufficiently indulged, it may guarantee bad criticism.[16]

Art works and cultural contexts ought to be treated as people should be, as individuals, not in multiples. Art works cannot be examined precisely with the tools of classification, with archetypal categories or mythic patterns. We all do indulge in categorizations of peoples using broad guidelines of types (some do it professionally), but we know, after all the general talk, that the only way to take human beings is one at a time. However interesting it may be to see how a given individual fits the patterns of various archetypal classifications in which he may belong, precise judgments concerning individual worth cannot rest with such classifications.

Likewise with the "deconstruction" of literary texts and social contexts. Nihilistic fragmentation of either will lead first to critical and cultural anarchy and then (since some continuity is necessary to create any context at all) to the attempt at the imposition of somebody's intellectual or political social order. And it will be precisely those with a loved and unique cultural context which does not fit the plan of the new millennialist society that will suffer.

III. Notes on Marxism and McLuhanism

i. Marx: Class as a Reductive Category

Rereading the *Manifesto* after more than twenty years since undergraduate days, I find the by now familiar monist compulsion lurking behind the equally familiar two-category *weltanschauung*:

> The history of all hitherto existing society is the history of class struggles.
> Freeman and slave, patrician and plebeian, lord and serf, guildmaster and journeyman, in a word; oppressor and oppressed, stood in constant opposition to one another, carried on an uninterrupted, now hidden, now open fight, a fight that each time ended, either in a revolutionary re-constitution of society at large, or in the common ruin of the contending classes.

"In a word; oppressor and oppressed" reveals the compulsion to simplify complex realities so as to create manageable categories. If close analysis of all hitherto existing social classes, of the infinitely fine gradations within classes, of the mobility that may have existed within or between classes, is inconveniently complicated for the creation of dualistic opposites, then the categories of analysis will have to be reduced:

> In the early epochs of history, we find almost everywhere a complicated arrangement of society into various orders, a manifold graduation of social rank. In ancient Rome we have patricians, knights, plebians, slaves; in the middle ages, feudal lords, vassals, guild-masters, journeymen, apprentices, serfs; in almost all of these classes, again, subordinate gradations.
> The modern bourgeois society that has sprouted from the ruins of feudal society, has not done away with class antagonisms. It has but established new classes, new conditions of oppression, new forms of struggle in place of the old ones.
> Our epoch, the epoch of the bourgeoisie, possesses, however, this distinctive feature; it has simplified the class antagonisms. Society as a whole is more and more splitting up into two great hostile camps, into two great classes directly facing each other; Bourgeoisie and Proletariat.

The inevitable question is, has "our epoch" simplified the struggle or has the author? I have seen this reductionism so often in my own primarily literary studies, this compulsion to simplify categories in the full existential reality so as to impose some dialectic intellectual synthesis, some precut pattern, that I cannot help doubting the precision of any analysis to come that begins this way.

Were there *really* manifold class gradations in "early epochs" or were there really but two—"oppressor and oppressed"—as now in our epoch? Marx wants it both ways. He asserts that things merely *seemed* complex, diverse (and in some ways beautiful) in the past only because the underlying ugly (and simple) exploitive struggle was veiled:

> The bourgeoisie, wherever it has got the upper hand, has put an end to all feudal, patriarchal, idyllic relations. It has pitilessly torn asunder the motley feudal ties that bound man to his "natural superiors," and has left remaining no other nexus between man and man than naked self-interest, than callous "cash payment." It

has drowned the most heavenly ecstasies of religious fervor, of chivalrous enthusiasm, of philistine sentimentalism, in the icy water of egotistical calculation. It has resolved personal worth into exchange value, and in place of the numberless indefeasible chartered freedoms, has set up that single, unconscionable freedom—Free Trade. In one word, for exploitation, veiled by religious and political illusions, it has substituted naked, shameless, direct, brutal exploitation.

The bourgeoisie has stripped of its halo every occupation hitherto honored and looked up to with reverent awe. It has converted the physician, the lawyer, the priest, the poet, the man of science, into its paid wagelaborers.

The bourgeoisie has torn away from the family its sentimental veil, and has reduced the family relation to a mere money relation.

Marx's ambivalence toward past epochs is clear; the scholar in Marx wants to admit that there have been contexts of beauty, of religion, of chivalric behavior, of work, and of family, worth having, illusions of some value. The fanatic to an idea scorns all illusions, except of course the promised millennial illusion of his own imagination:

Political power, properly so called, is merely the organized power of one class for suppressing another. If the proletariat during its contest with the bourgeoisie is compelled, by the force of circumstances, to organize itself as a class, if, by means of a revolution, it makes itself the ruling class, and, as such, sweeps away by force the old conditions of production, then it will, along with these conditions, have swept away the conditions for the existence of class antagonisms, and of classes generally, and will thereby have abolished its own supremacy as a class. (Sec. 2)

And the monist compulsion is fulfilled: manifold classes first reduced to two, and then finally to one, which of course by definition is no class. Thus the hated classes are gone, and there is wondrously no need for any State or political power, since Marx defines political power as "merely the organized power of one class for suppressing another. . ."

The detailed argument for the historical necessity of Marx's dialectic coming to pass, the inevitability of the triumph of the proletariat, is in *Capital*, and the classic refutation of the argument is the aforementioned Karl Popper's *The Open Society and its Enemies*. In *The Open Society* Popper distinguishes in a summary statement between Marx's power as an analyst of existing social institutions and the "poverty" of his "historicism," that is, of Marx's (anyone's) power of prophecy concerning historical "pattern":

> A closer view of Marx's successes shows that *it was nowhere his historicist method which led him to success, but always the methods of institutional analysis.* . .
>
> Nowhere in these analyses do the typical historicist 'laws of historical development', or stages, or periods, or tendencies, play any part whatever. On the other hand, none of Marx's more ambitious historicist conclusions, none of his 'inexorable laws of development' and his 'stages of history which cannot be leaped over', has ever turned out to be a successful prediction. Marx was successful *only* in so far as he was analysing institutions and their functions. And the opposite is true also: none of his more ambitious and sweeping historical prophecies falls within the scope of institutional analysis. Wherever the attempt is made to back them up by such an analysis, the derivation is invalid. Indeed, compared with Marx's own high standards, the more sweeping prophecies are on a rather low intellectual level. (P. 197)

As, for instance, the classless-society dream discussed above:

> The unity or solidarity of a class, according to Marx's own analysis, is part of their class consciousness, which in turn is very largely a product of the class struggle. There is no earthly reason why the individuals who form the proletariat should retain their class unity once the pressure of the struggle against the common class enemy has ceased. Any latent conflict of interests is now likely to divide the formerly united proletariat into new classes, and to develop into a new class struggle. (The principles of dialectics would suggest that a new antithesis, a new class antagonism, must soon develop. Yet, of course, dialectics is sufficiently vague and adaptable to explain anything at all, and therefore a classless society also, as a dialectically necessary synthesis of an antithetical development.) (P. 138)

Popper's refutations of various of Marx's assumptions occupy much of *The Open Society* and are serious responses to serious hypotheses of Marx. But finally Popper must say that "Marx's theory of classes must be considered as a dangerous oversimplification" (p. 116). And it is so not because Marx was not a scholar or humanist—he was both—but because of his monomania (called by Popper his "essentialism"), his compulsion to explain the whole reality with one archetypal key:

> Thus all thoughts and ideas would have to be explained by reducing them to the underlying essential reality, i.e., to economic conditions. This philosophical view is certainly not much better than any other form of essentialism. (P. 107)

If you don't have the key, say the essentialists, don't you dare argue with any of the keyholders:

> But don't wrangle with us so long as you apply, to our intended abolition of bourgeois property, the standard of your bourgeois notions of freedom, culture, law, etc. Your very ideas are but the outgrowth of the conditions of your bourgeois production and bourgeois property. (*Communist Manifesto*, sec. 2)

This is the customary sweeping arrogance of all those who have, in Swift's words, eaten of the "universal pickle" (see *A Tale of a Tub*, sec. 4). Or in Popper's more temperate prose:

> In a previous chapter, when dealing with 'Vulgar Marxism' I mentioned a tendency which can be observed in a group of modern philosophies, the tendency to unveil the hidden motives behind our actions. . . . Hegelianism does it by declaring the admissibility and even fertility of contradictions. But if contradictions need not be avoided, then any criticism and any discussion becomes impossible since criticism always consists in pointing out contradictions either within the theory to be criticized, or between it and some facts of experience. The situation with psychoanalysis is similar: the psycho-analyst can always explain away any objections by showing that they are due to the repressions of the critic. . . .
> Marxists, in a like manner, are accustomed to explain the dis-

agreement of an opponent by his class bias. . . . Such methods are both easy to handle and good fun for those who handle them. But they clearly destroy the basis of rational discussion, and they must lead, ultimately, to anti-rationalism and mysticism. (*The Open Society*, pp. 215–16)

Dialectic, whether Hegelian, Marxist, Freudian or other, is, as I have experienced it, just such oversimplification of the categories of discourse followed by the imposition of a monist synthesis. My remarks above and below are not intended to do much more than to show this methodology: the creation of dualistic categories which pretend to explain everything while really just giving new labelings to things from a new perspective. The perspective of economism (economics as fundamental law, societal life as manifestation of modes of production) is certainly a striking perspective worth examining. In so far as it is true, it should alter old perspectives; in so far as it is false, it should itself be altered. This is how things should happen, not how they do happen. Inertia in the status quo, dynamism in the new idea, can create irrational forces which can end in the destruction of one side or another, or both. It need not however be the rightness of the ideas impelling either side that determines victory, but the force marshaled by the adherents of either side. Marxism might conquer the world, but that would prove little about its dialectic, any more than a fistfight in the street determines the rightness of the view of either fighter.

When the authorities of a state and its opponents are disposed to see only two classes of people, whatever the two classes, their sort and the others, everyone must shudder, for there is no guarantee of any end to the purging for ideological purity on either side. I sensed as an undergraduate that *all* extreme political ideology, radical or reactionary, was dangerous for me, the immigrant's son with a deeply felt though fragile set of local contextual loves, that the only politics not dangerous to me would be that motivated by a humane will to make things a bit better day by day through small, tentative, piecemeal, pragmatic changes. "Ideas are a dime a dozen," I told myself then. "Many talk as if they know how to build a great society, or to write a beautiful book, but who can do it?" The proof is, alas, there only in the accomplishment, in the jewel of a beautiful book, in the jewel of a healthy social context, and jewels are rare. Humility, not arrogance, is all one can counsel concerning one's ideas, unless one is prepared to impose one's ideas with the barrel of a gun or the shout of a mob.

ii. "Media" and McLuhan: Imprecision as Archetype

Typical of the categorical mind in various of its manifestations is its one-way vision, its seeing the world in terms of my truth and your error, my rights and your obligations, my good friends and your evil clique. The full vision, of the limitations and pain of actual existence, of the inextricable dualisms of truth and error, good and evil, not only in others, but in ourselves, is paralyzing to the dialectical, the transcendental, the apocalyptic, or the millennialist compulsion. At the vulgarist level of the mass media, the compulsion is satisfied by the "unmasking" of various conspiracies which are keeping the audience from sundry utopias. At the level of a *Time* magazine, the omniscient voice tells all about the immediate past and oracles the distant future, baffled only by the immediate future. At the level of the *intellegentsia*, the reviewers in the journals too often bite at one another like dogs, and with all of the arrogance of gods, over issues largely metacritical.

"Media"—mass and elitist—overwhelmed me, as I suspect it does most, as a freshman undergraduate. Nurtured in the concept of the "well-rounded man," I was initially impressed that, say, a *Time* magazine seemed to offer so much cultured knowledge in so many areas and so quickly. Impressed too I was by the absolute certainty of tone of the "higher" journals. As the student becomes more knowledgeable in a few areas, he finds that *Time* cannot satisfy the demands of precision much beyond the undergraduate level in those areas, and thus, most likely, in most of the areas. The graduate student a few years later finds that most of the debates of the members of the various clubhouses in the higher journals consist usually of diametric oppositions, with the tone of certainty and arrogance the common denominator of both sides.

The most sobering lesson of all comes when one has worked one's way to a personal sense of some precision in a small area of knowledge, and finds how few really care for or about precision of analysis in that area, preferring rather the broad, the categorical, the reductive-dialectical, the archetypal, or the apocalyptic. Thus it is at all levels of media from the "lowest" to the "highest" that we can find ourselves engulfed in waves of arrogant propaganda, brainwash, or group-think of more or less subtlety. The "well-rounded" man works to "keep up" or "current" with the media at his level, but in fact often drowns in a passive reception of loads of largely imprecise material. The percentage of beautifully done, precisely done analyses in the mass media and other sorts of media is largely lost when the greatest part of the audience has not trained itself to care about the difference between precision and imprecision.

One can only counsel selectivity, caution, and humility: selectivity in choosing areas in which to work or to read where one has knowledge enough to exercise the critical spirit (that is, the accurate response to, and precise articulation of, the central attitudes implicit in a unique context); caution as a receiver in accepting proffered opinion in media whenever and wherever it is couched in terms of certainty and arrogance; humility as a metacritic in realizing that one's values, however imperative they may be for oneself, are but continuities within a context to others, a context which many, perhaps most, cannot share.

Such a realization and such caution comes easier perhaps to those who are somewhat "outsiders" to—Wimsatt would call it being in a relationship of some tension with—the given social context and the media involved with it. (The immigrant's son at the Midwestern American college such as I was may have that privilege as compensation for his disorientation.) Group or peer pressure creates short-term fashions or long-term mores that can be for better or worse in the continuity of the social context. The observer who would also be social or media critic must be sufficiently within the context to appreciate the nature and value of its continuities and sufficiently outside of it to understand that there are other continuities equally fine or limited (though different), and thus not be a dogmatist for or against the given context and its various media of expression.

With ideas such as the above, I came with anticipation to a reading of Marshall McLuhan's *Understanding Media* (1964) and *The Medium Is the Massage* (1967). I had run across a few of Professor McLuhan's literary essays, which I had found stimulating, and thought to find works on media which would focus issues precisely. It was a disappointment to find instead works of confused and confusing tonality, of arrogance mingled with irresolution, of exultation with despair, insight with opacity. McLuhan was predicting an electronic media revolution in society the nature of which was now inevitable, now not inevitable, now wholly desirable, now potentially loathsome. "Global Tribalism" was his term for the new society to come, and in his *The Medium Is the Massage (MM)*, he illustrates his vision by an absurd photograph of a primitive tribe listening to their witch doctor. He can't be serious! one exclaims. Are *we* being put upon, or is McLuhan putting himself on, expressing his own ambivalence toward—his yearning for and fear of—what he is predicting? What he seems to be saying, if there is no self-irony, is typical stuff of the categorical mind—a monomessage (the medium *is* the message; the medium not the content imposes, disposes; the given society is a creature of its media) and a reductive reading (or revealing) of History with the archetypal key (wheel was the key, type was the key, TV is the key), and all unfolding into a dubious millennial prophecy. There is the tone of infallibility, of the author knowing the truth latent beneath the appearances; the uninitiated focus on the trivial manifest content while the author has a lock on the subliminal effects of the key, in McLuhan's case the various media, which is all that is truly relevant.

Having the key means that one can indulge in such grand reveries as this:

Our habit of visualizing renders the literate Westerner helpless in the nonvisual world of advanced physics. Only the visceral and audile-tactile Teuton and Slav have the needed immunity to visualization for work in the non-Euclidean math and quantum physics. Were we to teach our math and physics by telephone, even a highly literate and abstract Westerner could eventually compete with the European physicists. (*Understanding Media*, p. 267)

The bookish Teuton as visceral and audile-tactile! What of the Italian who belches at his wine, sings in the street and pinches the girls? Is he not a candidate for Higher Physics on or off the telephone? Is the Middle or Far Easterner sufficiently nonvisual to compete? McLuhan's comment is either imprecise rubbish or revelation, and I opt for rubbish. The lead in theoretical physics in Eastern European countries can be explained as well by the rgior and precision of the elitist *gymnasium*. But, says the McLuhanite, this is only the superficial answer which looks only at the manifest content of a society, the 180° wrong answer. The "good" school, with its typographical, linear, visual, book emphasis, is actually a hindrance to higher physics. The theoretical justifications for such comments are in McLuhan's *Gutenberg Galaxy*—a more impressive book than *Understanding Media*—but McLuhan has become so confident of his ground that he will indulge in such loose talk, which is either useless or false unless so qualified as to make the whole effort questionable. The strategy is presumably to shake up imprecise established opinion by imprecise nonestablished opinion.

The strategy for *The Medium Is the Massage* is apparently to be even more provoking by being even more imprecise. Take note! he says: Family is obsolete, neighborhood is obsolete, nation is obsolete; Total Change is coming! (*MM*, pp. 14–16) Self is out, Age is out; Youth and Teamwork is in (pp. 100–101, 114, 123). Precision is out, "myth" and "participation mystique" are in (p. 114), and TV has "got it all on" (p. 125).

And yet he also says: "there is absolutely no inevitability as long as there is a willingness to contemplate what is happening" (p. 25), which is described as "our predicament, our electrically-configured whirl" (p. 150). And further: "Far from regarding technological change as inevitable, I insist that if we understand its components we can turn it off any time we choose. Short of turning it off, there are lots of moderate controls conceivable." (*New York Times Magazine*, 29 January 1967). Why these counterstatements? Why control something elsewhere depicted as so wonderful, so participatory, so self-immersible, so self-oblivious? Answer: because it is a consummation not so devoutly wished by McLuhan, if it doesn't turn out the way his millenialist desires have dreamt it. He knows that he does not like the history of the West in general since Gutenberg, and modern times in particular (see *The Mechanical Bride* and *The Gutenberg Galaxy*). He has some hopes that the electronics revolution may culminate in something like a pre-Gutenberg, even preliterate, mentality in humanity on a global scale (I share the same desire or nostalgia for my parents' peasant mentality; see above, p. 134–35). And he seems to feel that if he predicts it often and positively enough, it might even come to pass.

This thumbnail sketch of McLuhanism is intended only to make clear that I find at the base of the McLuhan System the same old ultimate tendency to dispose all of existence into reductive categories so as to create broad syntheses.[17] The global village at the end of the historical process is as much a millennial dream as Marx's classless society. It is another example of what Popper calls the "poverty of Historicism," where historical data is cut along designed patterns to achieve a preordained goal.

It need not be so in the criticism of media. One needs to take a manageable selection of works in areas in which one is knowledgeable and look at them closely, first intrinsically and then in the context of their social situation, and attempt to evaluate their continuity, coherence, and effectiveness within that context (which McLuhan does brilliantly again and again). One will expect to find, as with encounters with people (to return to my cliché), a percentage of excellence in every sort of medium and at every level from "low" to "high." One will find too that media manipulation and propaganda are enormous forces in the modern world, and that benign ends are not the likely results of malign forces.

McLuhan's intermittent sanguineness about the inevitable direction of or our ability to control media forces reads finally more like helplessness than confidence. What do we do in any case about media manipulation and its consequent evils in the short run as we wait for the spirit of youth and electronics to bring about the total change to mystic participation? How do we (should we want to? can we?) "turn off" the "controls" if we don't like what the prophetic screen is revealing to us? How indeed. Not, certainly—I would assert—by reading McLuhan, who is I think as confused as we are about these questions.

A case in point. "Freedom of the Press" and of the media in general is to most of us in Western cultures a "right" of mankind as inalienable as the rights to "life, liberty and the pursuit of happiness." The absoluteness of this right may be as fictitious as the others may be (see above, p. 139–40). Except that men may compact to agree on the necessary illusions of inalienable rights as equally beneficial to all the compactors, and in exchange for which they agree to inalienable obligations. But, as Simone Weil says:

> The notion of obligations comes before that of rights, which is subordinate and relative to the former. A right is not effectual by itself, but only in relation to the obligation to which it corresponds, the effective exercise of a right springing not from the individual who possesses it, but from other men who consider themselves as being under a certain obligation toward him. (*The Need for Roots*, p. 3)

There is no "right" to freedom of the press without concomitant obligations of the press. These obligations are certainly involved with the avoidance of conscious lying or manipulations to deprive others of their freedoms, their rights. And, as with the obligations of love (see above, pp. 131–32), these obligations of the press or other media of communication toward justice, equity, and amity are the crowning glory, the raison d'être of the freedom. It is not long however, given the human capacity for cupidity, in any free society before the subtle, necessary relationship between these rights and obligations is abused, as when media become big, profitable business or power vehicles for special interests. Such interests use media to promote these interests; competing interests create their own propaganda vehicles, and free interchange of ideas becomes more like random collisions between impenetrable half-truths. Liars and profiteers hide behind the First Amendment as gangsters hide behind the Fifth Amendment. So precious, so fundamental to the workings of our social compact is freedom of expression that we hesitate ever to punish exploitation of this freedom, just as we are willing to dismiss the prosecution of a hundred gangsters out of fear that one innocent man may suffer if Fifth Amendment protections are weakened. Yet one agrees only to protect the malefactors; one ought not to take the malefactors to one's bosom. Simone Weil finds our trepidations vexing:

> We all know that when journalism becomes indistinguishable from organized lying, it constitutes a crime. But we think it is a crime impossible to punish. What is there to stop the punishment of activities once they are recognized to be criminal ones? Where does this strange notion of nonpunishable crimes come from? It constitutes one of the most monstrous deformations of the judicial spirit. (Ibid., pp. 37–38)

But we have little to offer by way of answer or remedy. We know that expression is no more free than is trade under oligarchic manipulation. And we do not feel that the only answer to the offenses of one oligarchy need be those of another competing oligarchy. We do have antitrust laws in the direction of control of oligarchic manipulation of trade, however weak they are. It should be within the realm of possibility that the abuse of the obligations and the accountability of media to facts or the rights of others be subject to judicial review.

But be that as it may, my subject is not really the conscious, malicious manipulation of audiences for profit or power, but manifestations of the categorical mind, which imposes or tries to impose a one-way vision or group-think only because it is sure it is absolutely *right* about something or other. What is most in danger in a society deluged by mass media is the individual personality and its unique creative potential. To treat the individual casually in lauding the masses and team-work is to treat oneself casually. Yet McLuhan for all of his insight into the dangers, seems willing:

> Print technology created the public. Electric technology created the mass. The public consists of separate individuals walking around with separate, fixed points of view. The new technology demands that we abandon the luxury of this posture, this fragmentary outlook. . . .
> As new technologies come into play, people are less and less convinced of the importance of self-expression. Teamwork succeeds private effort. (*M.M.*, pp. 68–69, 123)

It is testimony to the force of theory that a man like McLuhan, who has loved unique literary contexts, gets to this juncture, where he is sitting, most uncomfortably I would think, with the brethren of the categorical mind who create systems and visions at the expense of individuals, exalt generalities and abstractions above unique contexts, and exchange new millenialist dogmas for the old existential realities.

Notes

1. Sumner on "rights":

> The notion of right is in the folkways. It is not outside of them, of independent origin, and brought to them to test them. . . . "Rights" are the rules of mutual give and take in the competition of life which are imposed on comrades in the in-group, in order that the peace may prevail there which is essential to the group strength.
> . . . The passion for equality, the universal use of contract, and the sentiments of humanitarianism are informing elements in modern society. Whence did they come? Undoubtedly they came out of the mores into which they return again as a principal of consistency. (*Folkways*, pp. 29, 39)

Vaihinger on "freedom":

We encounter at the very threshold of these fictions one of the most important concepts ever formed by man, the idea of *freedom*. . . . men have formed this important construct from immanent necessity, because only on this basis is a high degree of culture and morality possible. But this does not prevent our realizing that it is itself a logical monstrosity, a contradiction; in a word, only a fiction and not an hypothesis. For centuries liberty has been regarded not merely as an hypothesis but as an unassailable dogma. It then fell to the rank of a disputed hypothesis, and to-day it is already often regarded as an indispensable fiction. A bitter struggle was necessary before we attained our present attitude, which for a long while was far from general. On this modern view there is nothing in the real world corresponding to the idea of liberty, though in practice it is an exceedingly necessary fiction. (*The Philosophy of "As If,"* p. 43)

2. The following are typical of what one finds when one looks:

After being met with a fierce resistance, Freud's work gained considerable acceptance. Its impact on Western culture in the twenties and thirties is incalculable. The shock wave has now passed however, and close inspection of psychoanalysis must produce in all but its most devoted adherents considerable disappointment. Contemporary psychology and psychiatry would be far richer and far wiser if Freud had not been so wrong so often. These two sciences have learnt, at some cost, that there are no short-cuts. In most respects psychoanalysis has proved to be a hindrance to the development of these sciences. Many years of sustained work have had to be discarded and the plodding discipline of science reinstated. . . .

The poor quality of the evidence presented in the case of Little Hans is merely one illustration of the lax attitude shown by analysts in evaluating clinical data. (*Critical Essays on Psychoanalysis*, ed. Stanley Rachman [Oxford 1963]; from Rachman's "Introduction," pp. x, xii.)

We thus have the curious position that psychoanalysis is widely accepted among lay people and others untrained in psychology, ignorant of experimental methods and incapable of evaluating empirical evidence. On the other hand, we have a widespread rejection of psychoanalytic claims by those knowledgeable in psychology . . . . (H. J. Eysenck, "Psychoanalysis: Myth or Science?" in Rachman, *Critical Essays*, p. 67.)

. . . the bridge between psychoanalysis and science is exceedingly frail and likely to collapse under the lightest traffic . . . .

The key theories of psychoanalysis remain unverified. Given their *form*, their verification presents insurmountable difficulties. It is logically impossible to disprove a theory that explains all effects by a single cause . . . .

The Freudian psychology has shown itself highly adaptable to the needs of the *Zeitgeist* because psychoanalysis, like all monistic systems, is full of ambiguity, inconsistency, contradiction. (Lillian Blumberg McCall, "Freud and Scientific Truth," *Commentary*, April 1958, pp. 345–46.)

These from people within the disciple of psychology (see also the very witty and comprehensive attack, *The Case Against Psychoanalysis*, [New York, 1952] by Andrew Salter). George II. Mead in his *Mind, Self and Society* (Chicago, 1934) speaks of the "more or less fantastic psychology of the Freudian group" (p. 211). I quote in the text and in the notes below from a number of other social scientists and humanists.

3. McCall quotes Alfred Kroeber on the dubious procedures in Freud's *Totem and Taboo*:

"The above enumeration [the ten objections] has been compiled only far enough to prove the essential method of the work, which is to evade the painful process of arriving at a large certainty by the positive determination of smaller certainties and their unwavering addition, irrespective of whether each augments or diminishes the sum total of conclusions arrived at. For this method the author substitutes a plan of multiplying into one another fractional certainties—that is, more or less remote possibilities—without recognition that the multiplicity of factors must successively decrease the probability of the product. It is the old expedient of pyramiding the hypotheses, which, if theory had to be paid for like stocks or gaming cards, would be less frequently indulged in." ("Freud and Scientific Truth," p. 344)

Salter, *The Case against Psychoanalysis*, is very telling (and amusing) in demonstrating these procedures in Freud's theories of the Oedipus complex and wish-fulfillment in dreams.

4. See Henri Ellenberger, *Discovery of the Unconscious*, pp. 513, 515, 516, 520.

5. Could it be that psychoanalysis, as a therapy, will come to be replaced by other less laborious and more effective therapies? (Ibid., p. 525)

Barring some radical change of attitude among analysts, there is a serious possibility that the whole subject will take the road of phrenology and end as a curious derelict. (Rachman, *Critical Essays*, p. xi).

But as soon as it became evident—it did not for many years—that psychoanalysis failed as often as any other psychiatric treatment, the Freudians began to stress the "constitutional factor" in neurosis, and to insist that only philistines set any store by mere "results." (McCall, "Freud and Scientific Truth," p. 345.)
See also Richard LaPiere, *The Freudian Ethic* (New York, 1959), p. 70.

6. These larger issues are given what seems to me brilliant treatment in LaPiere's book cited in note 5 above; his pages 56–57, opening chapter 3, in fact state succinctly what my chapters 7 and 8 are laboring to say in different contexts:

There is no scientific evidence to support the Freudian idea that man is born with biologically provided urges, needs, or interests that set him at odds with the society in which he lives; there is no real reason to suppose that sex is the dominant, if submerged, force in the life of the individual; there is no reason, aside from Freud's assurances, to think that what a man does is not what it seems to be; and there is no evidence, aside from that adduced by Freud and his disciples in accordance with their interpretative system, that the child inevitably—or even ever—develops an Oedipus complex, followed by a castration complex or penis envy, and that he thereafter goes fumbling and stumbling through life with the balance between his id, his ego, and his superego ever precarious and ever subject to jeopardy. There is not even any scientific evidence that the concepts of id, ego, and superego represent actual components of the individual's psyche.
Neither is there any scientific evidence that man possesses a soul. Nor is there any

scientific reason for believing that there is a life after death. Nor is there any scientific method of validating the scientists' assumption that there is order in the universe. Nonetheless, men have acted and still do act as though they have souls and a future life and as though the world about them is governed by laws of nature or of God. Any by so acting they render these various ideas socially valid.

McCall is equally succinct in stating why Freudianism is not likely to have much social "validation" in the long run:

> There can be no conception of freedom and responsibility in a system that attributes the motivation of all human behavior to unconscious, irrational, and conflicting forces over which consciousness has virtually no control. ("Freud and Scientific Truth," p. 346)

7. I am not of course questioning the role of the psychological in literature and criticism; its importance is a mere truism. What is at question is the imposition of Freudian dogmatics (or any dogmatics) on the interpretation of literature and the other arts. For example, Coleridge's "Ancient Mariner" and "Kubla Khan," Poe's "City in the Sea," "Dreamland" and "Ulalume," really most of the work of both men, are conscious psychological self-dramatizations, and both authors often use a dream symbology, sometimes traditional, sometimes personal. The forms, *mythoi*, patterns of action, in both are dictated by the psychological states each wants to render. The important distinction to make is that Coleridge's poems and Poe's poems are consciously wrought symbolic allegories of the state of their souls or psyches, and invite close analysis on these terms. Insofar as the poems are successes, they need no other sort of outside analysis of their author's psychology. Insofar as they are failures, their shortcomings may then be considered in the light of the biographical and psychological data about the poem's author.

8. See my *The Rape of Cinderella*, pp. 224–28, for a fuller treatment of this subject.

9. "We must admit that the essence of the artistic function also remains inaccessible to psychoanalysis"—quoted in the Shapiro article cited in text below. Freud is treated with inordinate respect by great numbers of the *literati;* coming from the opposite direction are people like Hugh Kenner, "Tales from the Vienna Woods," in *Gnomon* (New York, 1958), Robert Graves ("the psychoanalytic racket," "the moronic spirit of psychoanalysis"), *Sewanee Review* (Autumn 1949) pp. 698–702, and Richard Gilman ("Psychoanalysis has thrown almost no light on art or artists or imagination in general") *New York Times Book Review*, 1 August 1976, p. 4.

10. Prof. Harold Bloom has recently spun four books from the threads of the Oedipus complex, save that he speaks of authoritarian literary Fathers and murderous literary Sons. The categorizing urge in these books, the weaver's hunger to swallow up authors, creates a web of imprecision with regard to separate texts.

11. Primitive man, according to Mircea Eliade (like Jung, a scholar of the archetypes and myths of religion), centered his whole life around ritualizing what he considered sacred archetypal patterns:

> . . . . the greater part of primitive man's actions were, so he thought, simply the repetition of a primeval action accomplished at the beginning of time by a divine being, or mythical figure. An act only had meaning in so far as it repeated a

transcendent model, an archetype. The object of that repetition was also to ensure the *normality* of the act, to legalize it by giving it an ontological status; it only became real in so far as it repeated an archetype. (*Patterns in Comparative Religion* [New York, 1966], p. 33)

Eliade on Freudianism and "historical materialism":

Indeed one of the major differences separating the people of the early cultures from people to-day is precisely the utter incapacity of the latter to live their organic life (particularly as regards sex and nutrition) as a sacrament. Psychoanalysis and historical materialism have taken as surest confirmation of their theses the important part played by sexuality and nutrition among peoples still at the ethnological stage. What they have missed, however, is how utterly different from their modern meaning are the value and even the function of eroticism and of nutrition among those peoples. For the modern they are simply physiological acts, whereas for primitive man they were sacraments, ceremonies by means of which he communicated with the *force* which stood for Life itself.(Ibid., p. 31)

12. See my *The Rape of Cinderella*, especially chapter 2 and pp. 123–24, 220–24, and 258 n. 7. I attempt in my second chapter to demonstrate in an essay on Milton's "Lycidas" (also an important "litmus" poem for Frye in his *Fables of Identity*) that the breath of scholarship into the "archetypal" images and patterns in the genre of pastoral elegy had not elicited a precise enough articulation of the specific body of attitudes impelling "Lycidas." I refer the reader to that essay (and of course to Frye's by way of comparison).

13. The difference between psychic analysis and literary analysis is pointed by this anecdote in Ellenberger's book:

Strangely enough, when Jung was asked to write an introduction for the third edition of the German translation of Joyce's *Ulysses*, he failed to recognize that this work was a modern counterpart to the *Odyssey*, even including its *Nekyia*. Jung was puzzled by the apparent nonsense of the book. It seemed to be some sort of interminable "tapeworm," and he felt that the novel could be read as easily backward as forward. These comments were published in a journal and irritated Joyce. It is unfortunate for Jung that this article was the sole piece of literary criticism he ever published. He often referred in his seminars to English, French, or German novels in which he found unexpected illustrations of his theories. (*Discovery of the Unconscious*, p. 222)

14. William K. Wimsatt, *Hateful Contraries* (Lexington, Ky., 1965), passim; idem, "Northrop Frye: Criticism as Myth" (English Institute lecture, 1965), in *Day of the Leopards* (New Haven, 1976), pp. 74–96, M. H. Abrams, "The Correspondent Breeze" (1957), in *English Romantic Poets*, ed. Abrams, (New York, 1962), pp. 49–51; idem, review of Frye's *Anatomy of Criticism*, *University of Toronto Quarterly*, (January 1959): 194–95. The following summarizes Abrams's position:

. . . standard archetypal criticism can be charged with blurring, if it does not destroy, the properties of the literary products it undertakes to explicate. A mode of reading that persists in looking through the literal, particular, and artful qualities of a poem in order to discover a more important ulterior pattern of primitive, general, and unintended meanings eliminates its individuality, and threatens to nullify even its status as a work of art. For the result of such reading is to collapse the rich diversity of individual works into one, or into a very limited number, of archetypal patterns, which any one poem shares not only with other poems, but with such unartful phenomena as myth, dreams, and the fantasies of psychosis. (*English Romantic Poets*, pp. 49–50)

For a more recent critique embracing the various sorts of "Structuralist" literary criticism, see David Hirsh, "Deep Structures and Shallow Metaphors," *Sewanee Review* 85 (Winter 1977): 153–166; especially pp. 158–59.

15. The whole "deconstructive" enterprise has for me a strange feeling of "déjà vu." I remember in the late fifties at Oxford University walking into a lecture of Prof. P. F. Strawson's out of curiosity concerning the philosophic school of linguistic analysis (out of Wittgenstein), which was then at its height of influence. The lecture presumed to demonstrate the essential meaninglessness of some work of Kant. And I remember thinking "If Kant falls, who can stand?" (Karl Popper was then the leading voice against the school.) It has been the burden of this book that nihilistic philosophy cannot obviate the *need* for meaning in the human will.

16. Cf. the debate concerning "deconstruction" between Professors M. H. Abrams, J. Hillis Miller, and Wayne Booth in *Critical Inquiry* (Spring 1977) 3: 405–47, and Denis Donoghue's review essay "Deconstructing Deconstruction" in *New York Review of Books*, 12 June 1980, pp. 37–41. Professors Rene Wellek and Cleanth Brooks ably defend their critical positions in Wellek, "The New Criticism: Pro and Contra," *Critical Inquiry* (Summer 1978): 4: 611–24, and Brooks, "The New Criticism," *Sewanee Review* (Fall 1979): 89: 592–607.

17. The topic has had brilliant treatment in the essays by various hands comprising *McLuhan: Pro and Con* (Baltimore, Maryland, 1968). Essays in this volume (ed. Raymond Rosenthal) which are especially pertinent to the themes of this book are those by Dwight Macdonald, Neil Compton, Elemire Zolla, Anthony Quinton, Richard Kostelanetz, Theodore Roszak, and James Carey. Quinton draws analogies between McLuhan's system and Marx's as examples of Popper's "poverty of historicism" and "reinforced dogmatism" (pp. 191–92). Carey labels the McLuhan system as "one more myth, one more illusion by which men can organize their lives," which is all right since "it is our illusions ultimately that make us human"; but he adds that "it is the quality of moral imagination contained in McLuhan's myth that is disquieting" (pp. 306–7). Macdonald's summation would be my own:

. . . he's a system-builder and so interested in data only as building stones; if a corner has to be lopped off, a roughness smoothed to fit, he won't hesitate to do it. This is one of the reasons his book is dull reading—it's just those quirky corners, those roughnesses that make actuality interesting. (P. 33)

9
Concluding Summary: Education to Humility

The categorical mind, the posture of exultant dualism, the millennial dream, the primal crime, and the cosmic consciousness all find their source in the hunger for the abstraction of archetypal universals out of experience. It is a spiritual hunger for knowledge of origins and destiny as natural and human as physical hunger. It is only the arrogant pretension that one has the archetype which everyone must follow that rankles, not the desire for such.

The universe remains mysterious as men fabricate systems of more or less consistency or continuity out of metacritical hypotheses or more or less "testability" (which hardly matters to the maker). It was Santayana's judgment (above, p. 48) that all explanation of the beyond, all metaphysics, is poetry. It is Karl Popper's judgment that all explanations of origins and destiny of *this* world of experience are ultimately also exercises in metaphysics (above, p. 141).

Darwinism, for instance—to complete the triad, Darwinism, Marxism, Freudianism, which has haunted the modern mind—Popper regards as "metaphysical because it is not testable. . . . Darwinism does not really *predict* the evolution of variety. It therefore cannot really *explain* it." (*The Philosophy of Karl Popper*, vol. 1, p. 136.) My undergraduate biological studies were dominated by George Gaylord Simpson's *The Meaning of Evolution* which preached that the flow of evolution was essentially random and therefore directionless and purposeless for the individual human being. Pierre Teilhard de

184

Chardin in his *Phenomenon of Man* preaches that evolution has a direction made evident by the birth of conscious thought in the universe, and further that

> the greatest revelation open to science today is to perceive that everything precious, active, and progressive originally contained in that cosmic fragment from which our world emerged, is now concentrated in and crowned by the noosphere. (P. 183)

The "noosphere" represents the ever-expanding consciousness in evolving man, including the ultimate consciousness of his immortal destiny. Popper would be as skeptical about Teilhard's faith in our destiny as he is about all forms of prophecy, but he is as much awed by the birth of conscious thought as Teilhard is, and deeply respectful of the products of the creative human consciousness (what he calls "World 3") including emphatically "myths and fictions" (*The Philosophy of Karl Popper*, vol. 1, p. 155). These products Popper asserts, are contexts of human value, and their values are—must be— imposed on the world of fact:

> *although history has no meaning, we can give it a meaning.* . . . Ultimately, we may say the same about the "meaning of life." It is up to us to decide what shall be our purpose in life, to determine our ends. (*The Open Society and Its Enemies*, vol. 2, p. 278)

Thus Popper is fundamentally in agreement with the philosophers of "illusion as value." He would respect Teilhard, as he respects Arnold Toynbee (see *The Open Society*, 2: 251–58) for "giving life a meaning," though he could not accept the idea that the "unity of mankind can never be established in fact except within a framework of the unity of the superhuman whole of which Humanity is a part" (*The Open Society*, 2: 258), which is the culminating vision of both Toynbee and Chardin.

We have noted earlier the similarly tempered skepticism concerning the absoluteness of *any* of man's various values and idealisms in, for instance—to select two from the list—Hans Vaihinger and William Graham Sumner. For Vaihinger the concept of "freedom" is a contradiction and a fiction, but an "indispensable" and "exceedingly necessary fiction," for "only on this basis is a high degree of culture and morality possible" (*The Philosophy of "As If,"* p. 43). For Sumner, the notions of "rights" and "right," "morality," "equality," indeed all humanitarianisms and idealisms, are but products of the "folk-ways," yet they are at the same time "conventionalizations which persist . . . the resultant of experiments and experience as to the devices by which to soften and smoothen the details of life. They are indispensable" (*Folkways*, p. 70).

Vaihinger would explain the indispensability of these concepts not only on the basis of the "softening of life's details" or the desire for a higher culture, but also on a biological basis, using the idea that conscious thought developed in evolution to serve the purposes of the "Life-will" of the organism, not as an end in itself or as a vehicle to know "truth" (*The Philosophy of "As If,"* p. xxx). Simone Weil would, contrarily, see the bedrock of human need not in the biological cell but in man's higher consciousness or "soul":

> The first of the soul's needs, the one which touches most nearly its eternal destiny, is order; that is to say, a texture of social relationships such that no one is compelled to violate imperative obligations in order to carry out other ones. (*The Need for Roots*, p. 10)

Both Weil and Vaihinger, one a theist, one not, postulate an absolutist base for the need of continuity, for limited orders, contexts, or "roots," there where certain principles can become imperative obligations, though in the one case the principles are seen as numinous, in the other as fictive. Whatever truth is in either position (and I am sympathetic to both), I have attempted in this book and in earlier books to draw out some of the implications of such philosophies of continuity for aesthetic, social, and ethical contexts.

It may be argued then—as the poets of chapter 2 do argue—that human need as expressed in aesthetic, social, and ethical contexts yearns toward the condition (as a limit) of coherence and richness of texture, so as to enable one to have a sense of beauty and grace within the context, to live with a sense of sufficient absoluteness or imperativeness to give meaning and value to one's life and loves. It is the condition, the order, the equilibrium, toward which the characters of *The Golden Bowl* yearn and somewhat achieve. The outer darkness of suspension in contrariety is not only "hateful" but self-defeating.

Nietzsche has the substance, but in his acidity perhaps not the tone, of the position of illusion as value:

> The will to appearance, to illusion, to deception . . . is deeper, "more metaphysical," than the will to truth. (*Werke* 14: 369, quoted in Vaihinger, *The Philosophy of "As If,"* p. 360)
>
> The mind has heretofore been too weak and too uncertain of itself to grasp a hypothesis as an hypothesis and, at the same time, to take it as a guide. (*Werke* 13: 139, Vaihinger, p. 354)
>
> In order to act you must believe in error and you will continue to behave in accordance with these errors even when you have recognized them to be errors. (*Werke* 12: 224, Vaihinger, p. 351)

Unamuno has the tone as well:

> We must needs believe in the other life, in the eternal life beyond the grave, and in an individual and personal life, in a life in which each one of us may feel his consciousness and feel that it is united, without being confounded, with all other consciousnesses in the Supreme Consciousness, in God; we must needs believe in that other life in order that we may live this life, and endure it, and give it meaning and finality. And we must needs believe in that other life, perhaps, in order that we may deserve it, in order that we may obtain it, for it may be that he neither deserves it nor will obtain it who does not passionately desire it above reason and, if need be, against reason.
>
> And above all, we must feel and act as if an endless continuation of our earthly life awaited us after death. . . . (*The Tragic Sense of Life* p. 258)

And it is largely of tone that this book has been speaking. We hunger for order and continuity and value with no absolute proofs for the existence of any given metaphysical order; we can only long for, hope for, have faith in such an order. The situation calls plainly for some sort of humility, not arrogance.

Now there is admittedly such a thing as the arrogance of humility. Pope's *Essay on Man* counsels humility everywhere with an omnipresent tone of arrogance, and from such inconsistency this book may suffer here and there. But it ought not to be confused with the arrogance of the fanatic, as Santayana has defined him:

> Trouble only arises when the dialectician represents his rational dreams as knowledge of existences, and the mystic his excusable raptures as the only way of life. (*Interpretations of Poetry and Religion*, p. 18)

Metacritical arrogance in the scientist, the social scientist, or the humanist, assuredly including the artist (as Lawrence, above), is provoking because the attitude promises so much more than it can give. G. H. Bantock beautifully summarizes T. S. Eliot's view of these matters:

> Society, indeed, can only be meaningfully and fruitfully understood by those who start from a proper appreciation of the individual human dilemma, not by those who ignore the paradoxes of life in favor of some abstract and unrealistic belief in the possibility of total harmony and adjustment. Man is born to live in unease, and that unease is bound to be reflected in any fruitful thinking about human problems. Eliot believed, of course, that society could be organized on better or worse lines; but the theme that haunts him is that even at best the life of the world will only be a travesty of what can be imagined. (*T. S. Eliot and Education*, pp. 35–36)

This is Unamuno's tragic sense of life and T. S. Eliot is, it seems to me, along with Unamuno, one of those fruitful thinkers who has that "proper appreciation of the individual human dilemma."

Eliot on the relation of one's metacritical positions to educational archetypes:

> So that until we all come to agree in our theology, our agree-

ment on educational questions can be only an agreement on what is possible and desirable for a particular society under the peculiar conditions of its place, time, and composition.

. . . the assertion that a man's religion is his private affair, that from the point of view of society it is irrelevant, may turn out in the end to lead to a situation very favourable to the establishment of a religion, or a substitute for religion, by the State. ("The Aims of Education," in *To Criticize the Critic*, pp. 113, 117)

It is not necessary for the reader to share Eliot's religious beliefs to share in his sense of the modern metaphysical dilemma and the dependency of questions of any real importance on one's metacriticism of life. All educational archetypes (to focus on the one issue) are products of other metacritical archetypes. Monolithic state education leans to enforced worship of the power that provides the archetype, and tends towards the obliteration of the individual, the local, and the regional (above, pp. 125–30) in favor of the state. Yet the individual forms his personal and social identity from a core context of loves of family and neighborhood, and his intellectual identity from his encounters with specific teachers and "books." The bright and eager student, the capable and willing teacher, and a few shared beautiful books or experiences: this is the radiant core context at the individual and local level for which all the organizational schema of the state for students, teachers, curricula, and methodology cannot compensate.

Eliot argues that the familial, social, and educational contexts should all reinforce one another through the continuity of a live religious tradition, a continuity which ultimately only the divine authority of a religion—illusory or not—can provide. Popper would argue that his sort of rational humanism (see *The Open Society*, 2:258) is a viable alternative as a principle of continuity. My emotional life swells with the conviction that Eliot is right, that humanism cannot provide the social cohesion that religion can; my rational life, however, wants very much to be open to the possibility that Popper's ideas might build a tolerable "open society" without the need for a fanatic statism as a substitute for religious belief.

One's conclusions concerning any important matter are likely to be similarly paradoxical at a sufficiently abstract level, given the infinite desires of the will and the limitations of the mind. And so one must educate oneself to humility sooner or later in life. Yet in this compromised situation, one has consolations: one's faith may be true, as the universe remains a stupendous mystery; one's cultural and ethical values, religious or otherwise, are lovely in a context that one may be able to hold onto; one can stay loyal to the ethical imperatives blessedly imposed by the continuities of that beloved context; and finally, one can examine other lovely and unique cultures and contexts with some measure of precision, tolerance, understanding and compassion.

Sensitivity to the continuities of other contexts, ethical, religious, aesthetic, social, is the soul of the critical spirit; the ability to articulate that sensitivity is the art of criticism. But the soul of a man cannot (should not) be encompassed by the critical spirit; the will demands more, and a man's soul is perhaps defined by his strength of will to believe, to value, and to love:

> Over-beliefs in various directions are absolutely indispensable. We should treat them with tenderness and tolerance so long as they are not intolerant themselves. As I have elsewhere written, the most interesting and valuable things about a man are usually his over-beliefs. (William James, *The Varieties of Religious Experience*, p. 515)

The term over-beliefs is somewhat awkward and inelegant as, I would say, James attempts to balance his theism (above, p. 18) with the counterweight of his rational skepticism. It is always hard to do justice to delicately poised and paradoxical feelings and attitudes concerning issues that lie deep in the heart. But the attempt is laudatory, this concern for honesty and precision in the articulation of complex passional attitudes. It is a question of tone rather than substance, as it is a question of tone with most issues and contexts of real importance. And so, in the words of James's conclusion to his "The Will to Believe"

No one of us ought to issue vetoes to the other, nor should we bandy words of abuse. We ought, on the contrary, delicately and profoundly to respect one another's mental freedom: then only shall we bring about the intellectual republic; then only shall we have that spirit of inner tolerance without which all our outer tolerance is soulless; then only shall we live and let live, in speculative as well as in practical things.

This is how it should be, not how it is. And it may be that arrogance, imprecision, and intolerance have tragically an activist's edge over their opposites. Yet after the given local Armageddon a new context can only resurrect the humble losers, and with them a new faith in a new poetry. Such is at least one continuous story in the history of the human heart.

Bibliography

Abrams, Meyer H. "Anatomy of Criticism." *University of Toronto Quarterly* 28 (January 1959): 194–95.

———. "The Correspondent Breeze." In *English Romantic Poets*, edited by M. H. Abrams. New York: Oxford University Press, 1962.

———. "The Deconstructive Angel." *Critical Inquiry* 3 (Spring 1977): 425–38.

Aron, Raymond. *Main Currents in Sociological Thought*. New York: Basic Books, 1967.

Auden, W. H. *Selected Poetry of W. H. Auden*. New York: Random House, 1959.

Bantock, G. H. *T. S. Eliot and Education*. New York: Random House, 1969.

Benedict, Ruth. *Patterns of Culture*. Boston: Houghton Mifflin Co., 1959.

Bewley, Marius. *The Complex Fate*. New York: Gordian, 1967.

Blackmur, R. P. *Form and Value in Modern Poetry*. New York: Doubleday, 1957.

Blake, William. *Poetry and Prose of William Blake*, edited by Geoffrey Keynes. London: The Nonesuch Press, 1932.

Booth, Wayne. "Preserving the Exemplar." *Critical Inquiry* 3 (Spring 1977) 407–23.

Brooks, Cleanth. "The New Criticism." *Sewanee Review* 89 (Fall 1979) 592–607.

Bryan, W. F. and Dempster, Germaine. *Sources and Analogues of Chaucer's Canterbury Tales*. Chicago: University of Chicago Press, 1941.

Cavitch, David. *D. H. Lawrence and the New World*. New York: Oxford University Press, 1969.

Chase, Richard. *Walt Whitman Reconsidered*. New York: William Sloane, 1955.

Clair, J. A. *The Ironic Dimension in the Fiction of Henry James*. Pittsburg, Pa.: Duquesne University Press, 1965.

Clarke, Colin. *River of Dissolution*. New York: Barnes and Nobles, 1969.

Coleridge, Samuel Taylor. *Selected Poetry and Prose*. New York: Random House, 1951.

Conrad, Joseph. *The Portable Conrad*. New York: Viking Press, 1952.

Cooley, Charles Horton. *Social Organization*. New York: Scribner, 1916.

Crane, Hart. *The Collected Poems*. New York: Liveright, 1933.

Crews, Frederick. *The Tragedy of Manners*. New Haven, Conn.: Yale University Press, 1958.

Daleski, H. M. "The Duality of Lawrence." *Modern Fiction Studies* 5 (1959): 3–18.

Donoghue, Denis. "Deconstructing Deconstruction." *New York Review of Books* 12 June 1980, pp. 37–41.

Dostoevski, Fëdor. *The Brothers Karamazov*. Translated by Constance Garnett. New York: Random House, 1943.

Durkheim, Emile. *Selected Writings*. Cambridge: Cambridge University Press, 1972.

Edel, Leon. *Henry James: The Master*. Philadelphia: Lippincott, 1972.

Eliade, Mircea. *Patterns in Comparative Religion*. New York: New American Library, 1963.

Eliot, T. S. *After Strange Gods*. New York: Harcourt, Brace and Co., 1934.

———. *Collected Poems*. Harcourt, Brace and Co., 1963.

———. *Notes towards the Definition of Culture*. New York: Harcourt Brace Jovanovich, 1949.

———. *To Criticize the Critic*. New York: Farrar, Straus, 1965.

Ellenberger, Henri. *The Discovery of the Unconscious*. New York: Basic Books, 1970.

Eysenck, H. J. "Psychoanalysis: Myth or Science?" In *Critical Essays on Psychoanalysis*. Oxford: Oxford University Press, 1963.

Fielding, Henry. *Tom Jones*. New York: Random House, 1943.

Freud, Sigmund. *The Basic Writings of Sigmund Freud*. New York: Random House, 1939.

————. *The Complete Psychological Works of Sigmund Freud*. London: Hogarth Press, ongoing.

Friedman, Alan. "The Other Lawrence." *Partisan Review* 37 (1970): 239–53.

Friedman, Paul. "*The Bridge:* A Study in Symbolism." *Psychoanalytic Quarterly* 21 (1952): 49–80.

Fromm, Erich. *The Forgotten Language*. New York: Holt, Rinehart, 1951.

Frost, Robert. *Complete Poems of Robert Frost*. New York: Holt, Rinehart and Winston, 1949.

Frye, Northrop. *Anatomy of Criticism*. Princeton, N. J.: Princeton University Press, 1957.

————. *Fables of Identity*. New York: Harcourt, Brace and Co., 1963.

Gibran, Jean, and Gibran, Kahlil. *Kahlil Gibran*. New York: New York Graphic Society, 1974.

Gibran, Kahlil. *Broken Wings*. New York: Bantam, 1968.

————. *The Earth Gods*. New York: Alfred A. Knopf, 1931.

————. *The Forerunner*. New York: Alfred A. Knopf, 1920.

————. *The Garden of the Prophet*. New York: Alfred A. Knopf, 1933.

————. *Jesus, Son of Man*. New York: Alfred A. Knopf, 1928.

————. *The Madman*. New York: Alfred A. Knopf, 1918.

————. *The Prophet*. New York: Alfred A. Knopf, 1923.

————. *Sand and Foam*. New York: Alfred A. Knopf, 1926.

————. *A Second Treasury of Kahlil Gibran*. New York: Citadel Press, 1962.

————. *Secrets of The Heart*. New York: New American Library, 1973.

————. *A Treasury of Kahlil Gibran*. New York: Citadel Press, 1951.

————. *The Wanderer*. New York: Alfred A. Knopf, 1932.

Gilman, Richard. "Creativity." *New York Times Book Review* 1 August 1976, p. 4.

Goldberg, S. L. "*The Rainbow:* Fiddlebow and Sand." *Essays in Criticism* 11 (October 1961): 418–34.

Graves, Robert. "A Motley Hero." *Sewanee Review* 57 (Autumn 1949): 698–702.

Hall, Donald. "Interview With Ezra Pound." *Paris Review* 28 (1962): 22–51.

Hanna, Suhail. "Gibran and Whitman: Their Literary Dialogue." *Literature East and West* 7: 174–98.

Hartsock, Mildred. "Unintentional Fallacy: Critics and *The Golden Bowl.*" *Modern Language Quarterly* 35 (1974): 272–88.

Hawi, Khalil. *Kahlil Gibran.* Beirut: American University Press, 1963.

Hirsh, David. "Deep Structures and Shallow Metaphors." *Sewanee Review* 85 (Winter 1977): 153–66.

Horton, Philip. *Hart Crane: The Life of an American Poet.* New York: Norton, 1937.

Hough, Graham. *The Dark Sun.* New York: Macmillan Co., 1957.

James, Henry. *The Golden Bowl* [1904]. New York: Evergreen, 1959.

James, William. *The Varieties of Religious Experience.* New York: Collier Books, 1947.

―――. "The Will to Believe." In *Essays on Faith and Morals.* London: Longmans, Green, 1947.

Jarrell, Randall. *Poetry and the Age.* New York: Alfred A. Knopf, 1953.

Johnson, Samuel. *Selected Writings,* edited by B. Bronson. New York: Rinehart, 1958.

Jones, Ernest. *Hamlet and Oedipus* [1910]. New York: Norton, 1949.

Kanfer, Stefan. "But Is It Not Strange . . . That the Prophet Is Still Popular?" *New York Times Magazine,* 25 June 1972, pp. 8–9ff.

Keats, John. *Complete Poetry and Selected Prose.* New York: Random House, 1951.

Kenner, Hugh. "Tales From the Vienna Woods." In *Gnomon.* New York: McDowell, Obolensky, 1958.

Kimball, Jean. "Henry James's Last Portrait of a Lady." *American Literature* 28 (1957): 449–68.

Krook, Dorothea. *The Ordeal of Consciousness in Henry James.* Cambridge: Cambridge University Press, 1962.

LaPiere, Richard. *The Freudian Ethic*. New York: Duell, Sloan and Pearce, 1959.

Lawrence, D. H. "The Crown." In *Phoenix II*. London: Heinemann, 1968.

———. *The Rainbow*. New York: Viking, 1961.

Lentricchia, Frank. *After the New Criticism*. Chicago: University of Chicago Press, 1980.

———. *The Gaiety of Language*. Berkeley, Calif.: University of California Press, 1968.

McCall, Lillian B. "Freud and Scientific Truth." *Commentary*, April 1958, pp. 343–46.

McLuhan, Marshall. *The Gutenberg Galaxy*. Toronto: University of Toronto Press, 1962.

———. *The Mechanical Bride*. New York: Vanguard Press, 1951.

———. *The Medium Is the Massage*. New York: Bantam Books, 1967.

———. *Understanding Media*. New York: McGraw Hill, 1964.

Malinowski, Bronislaw. "On the Oedipus Complex" and "On the Social Functions of Religion." In *Theories of Society*, edited by Talcott Parsons et. al. New York: Free Press, 1961.

Marx, Karl. *The Communist Manifesto*. Translated by Samuel Morse [1888]. Chicago: Henry Regnery Co., 1950.

Mead, George H. *Mind, Self and Society*. Chicago: University of Chicago Press, 1934.

Meyers, J. "D. H. Lawrence and Homosexuality." In *D. H. Lawrence: Novelist, Poet, Prophet*. New York: Harper and Row, 1973.

Miller, J. Hillis. "The Critic as Host." *Critical Inquiry* 3 (Spring 1977): 439–47.

Mizener, Arthur. "The Spoils of Fawns." *New Republic*, 18 August 1952, pp. 17ff.

Moore, G. E. *Ethics*. London: Oxford University Press, 1912.

Moynahan, Julian. *The Deed of Life*. Princeton, N. J.: Princeton University Press, 1963.

Naimy, Mikhail. *Kahlil Gibran*. New York: Philosophical Library, 1950.

Naimy, Nadeem. *Mikhail Naimy: An Introduction*. Beirut: American University Press, 1967.

Nassar, Eugene Paul. *An Anatomy of Figuration* Philadelphia: University of Pennsylvania Press, 1965.

―――. *The Cantos of Ezra Pound: The Lyric Mode*. Baltimore, Md.: Johns Hopkins Press, 1965.

―――. *The Rape of Cinderella: Essays in Literary Continuity*. Bloomington, Ind.: Indiana University Press, 1970.

Neider, Charles. *The Frozen Sea*. New York: Oxford University Press, 1948.

Novak, Michael. "The Family Out of Favor." *Harper's*, April 1976, pp. 37–46.

Parsons, Talcott et. al., eds. *Theories of Society*. 2 vols. New York: Free Press, 1961.

Plato. *The Republic*. New York: Random House, n.d.

Poe, Edgar Allan. *Selected Prose and Poetry*. New York: Rinehart, 1950.

Popper, Karl. *Conjectures and Refutations*. New York: Basic Books, 1962.

―――. *The Open Society and Its Enemies*. 2 vols. Princeton, N. J.: Princeton University Press, 1963.

―――. *The Philosophy of Karl Popper*. 2 vols. LaSalle, Ill.: Open Court, 1974.

Pound, Ezra. *The Cantos: 1–117*. New York: New Directions, 1970.

―――. *Personae*. New York: New Directions, 1949.

Rachman, Stanley. *Critical Essays on Psychoanalysis*. New York: Pergamon Press, 1963.

Rosenthal, Raymond. *McLuhan: Pro and Con*. Baltimore, Md.: Penguin Books, 1968.

Ross, Charles L. "The Revisions of the Second Generation in *The Rainbow*." *Review of English Studies* 107 (1976): 277–95.

Sale, Roger. "The Narrative Technique of *The Rainbow*." *Modern Fiction Studies* 5 (Spring 1959): 29–38.

Salter, Andrew. *The Case Against Psychoanalysis*. New York: Citadel, 1952.

Samuels, Charles. *The Ambiguity of Henry James*. Champaign: University of Illinois 1971.

Santayana, George. *Interpretations of Poetry and Religion*. New York: Scribners, 1900.

———. "Shelley" In his *Winds of Doctrine*. New York: Harper and Brothers, 1957.

Sears, Robert R. *Survey of Objective Studies of Psychoanalytic Concepts*. New York: Social Science Research Council, 1943.

Sears, Sallie, *The Negative Imagination*. Ithaca, N. Y.: Cornell University Press, 1968.

Shapiro, Karl. "The Meaning of the Discarded Poem." In *Poets at Work*. New York: Harcourt, Brace, 1948.

———. *Start With the Sun*. Lincoln, Nebr.: University of Nebraska Press, 1960.

Shapiro, Meyer. "Leonardo and Freud." *Journal of the History of Ideas* 17 (April 1956): 147–78.

———. "Shelley." In his *Winds of Doctrine*. New York: Harper and House, 1951.

Sherman, Stuart P. "The Aesthetic Idealism of Henry James." In *The Question of Henry James*, edited by F. Dupee. New York: Henry Holt and Co., 1945.

Simpson, George G. *The Meaning of Evolution*. New Haven, Conn.: Yale University Press, 1960

Spilka, Mark. "Lawrence Up-Tight." *Novel* 4 (Spring 1971): 252–67.

Stevens, Wallace. *The Collected Poems of Wallace Stevens*. New York: Alfred Knopf, 1955.

Sumner, William Graham. *Folkways*. Boston: Ginn, 1940.

Swift, Jonathan. *Gulliver's Travels and Other Writings*. New York: Random House, 1958.

Teilhard de Chardin, Pierre. *The Phenomenon of Man*. New York: Harper and Row, 1961.

Thomas, Dylan. *The Poems of Dylan Thomas*. New York: New Directions, 1952.

Thomas, W. I. "The Four Wishes and the Definition of the Situation." In *Theories of Society*, edited by Talcott Parsons et. al. New York: Free Press, 1961.

Unamuno, Miguel de. *The Tragic Sense of Life*. Translated by J. E. C. Flitch. New York: Dover, 1951.

Vaihinger, Hans. *The Philosophy of "As If."* Translated by C. K. Ogden. London: Routledge, 1935.

Ward, J. A. "The Ambiguities of Henry James." *Sewanee Review* 83 (1975): 39–60.

Weil, Simone. *The Need for Roots.* Translated by A. Wills. New York: Harper and Row, 1971.

Weinstein, Philip. *Henry James and the Requirements of the Imagination.* Cambridge, Mass.: Harvard University Press, 1971.

Wellek, Rene. "The New Criticism: Pro and Contra." *Critical Inquiry* 4 (Summer 1978): 611–24.

Whicher, Stephen. "Whitman's Awakening to Death." In *The Presence of Walt Whitman.* New York: Columbia University Press, 1962.

Whitman, Walt. *Leaves of Grass.* New York: Rinehart, 1949.

———. *Leaves of Grass. The First (1855) Edition.* New York: The Viking Press, 1959.

Williams, William Carlos. *Selected Poems.* New York: New Directions, 1969.

Wilson, Edmund. *The Triple Thinkers.* New York: Farrar Straus, 1939.

Wimsatt, William K. *The Day of the Leopards.* New Haven, Conn.: Yale University Press, 1976.

———. *Hateful Contraries.* Lexington, Ky.: University of Kentucky Press, 1965.

Wordsworth, William. *Selected Poetry and Prose.* New York: Random House, 1950.

Wright, W. F. *The Madness of Art.* Lincoln, Nebr.: University of Nebraska Press, 1962.

Yeats, William Butler. *Collected Poems.* New York: Macmillan Co., 1958.

Yeazell, Ruth B. *Language and Knowledge in the Late Novels of Henry James.* Chicago: University of Chicago Press, 1976.

Young, Barbara. *This Man from Lebanon.* New York: Alfred A. Knopf, 1945.

Index

201